OUR
SOULS
AT
WORK

HOW GREAT LEADERS LIVE THEIR FAITH IN THE GLOBAL MARKETPLACE

Mark L Russell, Editor

Contributors:
Max Anderson, Mo Anderson, Dennis Bakke,
Corey Bell, Spencer Brand, Teal Carlock, Ben Chatraw,
Howard Dahl, Ken Eldred, Katherine Foo,
Dave Gibbons, Bonita Grubbs, Scott Harrison,
Henry Kaestner, George F. Kettle, Blake Lingle,
Brian Lewis, Steve Lynn, Ed Meese,
Matthew McCreight, Jeffrey Metzner, David W. Miller,
David Morken, Wendy Murphy, Blake Mycoskie,
Dennis Pemberton, Steve Reinemund,
Jeffrey A. Russell, Mark L. Russell, Rick Schneider,
Tyler Self, Harri Sundvik, Fonny Surya, John Tyson,
Bonnie Wurzbacher, Steve Wurzbacher, and Kim Yerino

russell
media

Boise, Idaho

Published by Russell Media
Boise, Idaho
www.russell-media.com

Additional editorial work done by Sandi Funkhouser, Laurie Russell, Andrea Smith, Nicole Wong, and Killian Creative, Boulder, Colorado (www.killiancreative.com).

Cover, graphic design, and layout by Drew Steffen

ISBN # 978-0-578-03989-3

Printed in the United States of America

18 17 16 15 14 13 12 11 10   1 2 3 4 5 6 7 8 9 10 11 12

CONTENTS

BALANCE

DISCIPLINES

RELATIONSHIPS

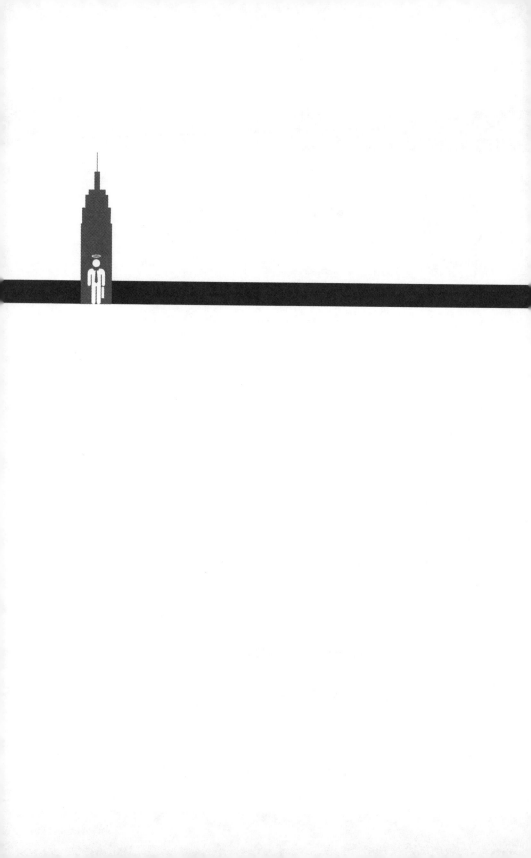

OUR SOULS AT WORK

FOREWORD

BY DAVE GIBBONS

(bio p. 255)

FOREWORD

It was the day of my mother's funeral; the day every child dreads and has nightmares about. It actually happened. As a second-year university student, I received a phone call that my mom was killed in a hit-and-run accident.

In the memorial service, I sat in disbelief as the room filled with family and friends. My father did not attend because he had recently finalized the divorce and remarried. It would have been awkward for him. It was my sister, my brother, and myself on the front row looking at my mom lying in a casket. The moment was surreal, accentuated by utter terror that Mom was gone. My mother had worked and sacrificed so much for us. She once said, "The only reason I live is for you children." Since the divorce, Mom's life had spiraled out of control. Her American dream had become a living nightmare. The house, swimming pool, new cars, boats, and trips didn't mean much to her after she and dad went their separate ways.

In the midst of the pain and what seemed to be a funeral service in slow motion, I felt I heard God saying to me, "Dave, on this earth there are things that are temporal and things that are eternal. The things that you desire don't mean much in light of eternity. I want you to give yourself completely to me and focus your life to serve me."

I translated that to mean God wanted me to go into ministry. This would be full surrender! In my mind, full surrender was full-time dedication to serving God as a pastor in a church not in a "secular" business in the world. Reluctantly, and with great resignation, I told God, "Okay, I will do it." At that moment, my journey to understanding what God meant had begun, while at the same time, an inner sense that I had a calling to business grew. I tried to quiet the conviction, but a deep inner conflict kept growing. I didn't know what to do with these seemingly incongruous feelings. How could I serve God fully other than as a minister? I buried this calling to business as a "worldly" or "secular" desire that I had to squash in order to stay obedient to what I thought was the true calling of full-time ministry. The spiritual leaders in my life told me that this ministerial calling was the highest and truest calling of all.

The Great Divide

Now, almost thirty years later, I think I have a fuller understanding of what God was trying to say to me as a young, passionate activist. The spiritual context I grew up in was a black and white environment. In an age of relativism, clear black and white posturing—theologically or politically—was common. The gravitational pull to simplicity and dogmatism seemed reactionary to what many feared was "liberalism" or "secularism" creeping into the church. Absolutes and clear lines of distinction were craved by a generation whose tenets of faith were being challenged by society.

The tone of spiritual conversation frequently drew upon war metaphors. While I know this is how Paul spoke in the New Testament, there are other metaphors of love and community that are also used. Again, not to condemn this generation's pursuit of Jesus, but I believe this is how the current rhetoric was shaped when it came to being fully surrendered to Jesus. In fact, I remember asking the senior minister one time, "Is everything so black and white in the Bible?" He said, "Yes."

What does this mean to those who are called to serve God outside of the church, or other than as traditional ministers?

Quite frankly, there was a difference for us between those who gave up all to go into "full-time ministry" and those who simply provided support to us in "full-time ministry." The secular and the sacred were distinct categories. Moreover, faith and work, while discussed, never really converged. Unfortunately, those who had regular nine-to-five jobs weren't really doing sacred work unless they served in the church. Is it any wonder that those who are not pastors only feel appreciated for their financial gifts and not for who they are as people?

In the global shifting that is going on today, the concerns are commonly economic and political in nature. However, the biggest concern should be the under-utilization of the human resources in our midst, those who comprise the church we go to every Sunday. There is a need for the priesthood, the body of Christ to arise. The normal every day businessperson, mother, student, worker need to see themselves at the frontline of what God is doing in the world. They should not be simply following the pastors; they are the ones called to lead.

The truth is that faith and work do intersect. In fact, all is sacred to God. Paul says, "Whether you eat or drink, or whatever you do, do all to the glory of God" (1 Corinthians 10:31 ESV). The highest calling is not being a pastor but becoming all God called you to be, namely a person who glorifies God in all you do.

The word *glory* conveys the idea of beauty. So as we do good work that reflects God's character graciously, purely, morally, ethically, creatively, and excellently, we unleash his beauty. People see God. Our work is a way to worship God. It has intrinsic value and can demonstrate God's character when we do *good* work. Faith and work are to be seamless. Work is an expression of our life in Christ. Separating the two is like separating *being* from *doing*. How do you know who you are *being* without considering what you are *doing*—or the fruit you are producing your life?

I am genuinely thrilled about the wisdom made available in this book, *Our Souls at Work*. A new priesthood is rising up that must understand who they really are and who they are called to become. This book will provide needed guidance and an astute perspective into how the Kingdom of God can be made relevant to all people at all times in all places. My hope is this book will catalyze the new prophets that aren't just concerned about a single bottom line, but rather a *multiple* bottom line. It's a group who doesn't only want to make a profit, but aims to make a difference! It's a wave of global leaders who aren't going to let pastors have all the fun. It's a growing movement of zealots who see themselves on the front lines of God's campaign, no longer confined to warming the bench on Sunday mornings. This is a generation of leaders who know they're called to do more than give money, but everything they have. They are not going to miss out on one of the greatest moments in history to be alive!

My prayer, as you read this book, is that the Holy Spirit will give you a clear vision of who you are as a passionate worshipper unleashing the beauty of God in all that you do at work, at home, in the church, and in the world at large. You can't separate what you do from who you are. Your work *is* your worship. So worship God with all your heart, soul, mind, and strength. Unleash his beauty beyond the four walls of your church and into all of the domains you serve in the world.

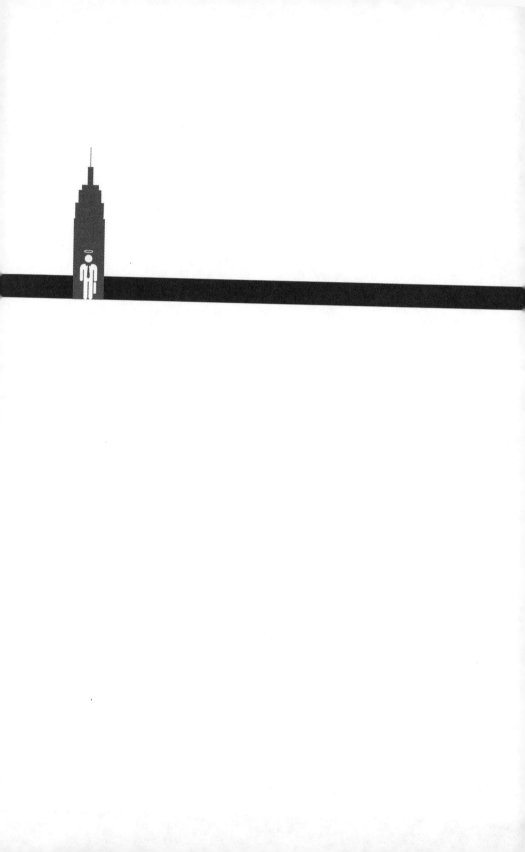

OUR SOULS AT WORK

INTRODUCTION

BY MARK L RUSSELL
(bio on p. 265)

INTRODUCTION

From Mumbai to Manhattan, from Bangkok to Boise, and from Athens to Atlanta, every morning people wake up and go to work. Likewise, all over the world people use their weekends to worship God. Very rarely is there a connection between these two activities, producing an enormous gap between our work and our worship. This book is about bridging that gap.

If you're like me, when something hurts you cannot stop thinking about it. When times are tough, it's difficult to think about anything other than the present challenge. Right now, the economy is posing an enormous challenge for many people around the world. Questions abound. What happened that caused this crisis? Where is it going? What is it doing? What will our collective future be like?

For many of us, the economic downturn at the end of the first decade of the twenty-first century came out of nowhere and left us wondering what was going on. As we have dug up answers, we haven't always liked what we have found. Stories of exploitation and greed have been uncovered, causing a lot of us to conclude that business is dirty—or at best, a necessary evil. Talk of business in a positive light by spiritually minded people has become rare indeed. Little is known or discussed regarding how we should relate our weekend faith with our daily work lives.

Churches have not been overly helpful in bringing faith to the work-world for a few reasons. In the early 90s, it became widely acknowledged among clergy that the primary reason people criticized and avoided church was that they felt churches just wanted their money. This was based in no small part on the several famous televangelist embezzlement schemes of the 1980s. Images of Tammy Faye Baker's mascara running down her face haunted people. "Churches are after my money," they thought. Not wanting to hinder church attendance, churches avoided the topic of finances, and by correlation, issues surrounding business and the workplace. Churches were not too concerned about avoiding such topics since they were never particularly comfortable addressing them in the first place.

One reason for this original lack of comfort is that many clergy have never worked in the marketplace and feel ill at ease or even intimidated discussing it. Subconsciously or intentionally they avoid any direct teaching and conversation on business matters, preferring to speak and teach on what they know best.

There are other clergy who once worked in the marketplace, but felt God had called them out of the marketplace into strictly church-related ministry—therefore their priority and attention is directed solely at "church-related ministry."

While God undoubtedly does call numerous people to leave their marketplace work, the subtle impression (and sometimes not-so-subtle teaching) presented by many of these clergy is that working in the church is spiritually superior to working in the marketplace. As a result, generally speaking, churches have not helped their members to understand the relevance of faith in regards to their work, something most people spend the majority of their waking hours doing.

Even with the surge in interest around the global economy, the silence of the church has been deafening. However, this is a strategic opportunity for us all to step back and look more closely at our work through the filter of our faith. The good news is that many people have done this through the years and we have the opportunity to build on their experiences.

In February 2007, my brother Jeff was a first-year student in the Yale University School of Management (SOM). The Yale SOM Christian Fellowship approached Professor David W. Miller, the Executive Director of the Yale Center for Faith & Culture at Yale Divinity School, and teacher of a popular course, "Business Ethics: Succeeding without Selling Your Soul," comprised of both SOM and Divinity School Students. Though now on the faculty of Princeton University, Miller served as an advisor and mentor to the SOM Christian Fellowship group and, drawing on his network of CEO friends, helped them put together a conference called "Believers in Business." Initially, the conference was intended for MBA students from Yale, but soon it attracted nationwide interest and MBA students from around the country attended. I was, at the time, a PhD student at Asbury Seminary, working on a dissertation focused on business from a theological and missional perspective. I traveled up to the conference and was one of the few non-MBA students there.

Great speakers and business executives like Steve Reinemund, Dennis Pemberton, Ken Eldred, Mo Anderson, Steve Lynn, David Miller, and others gave the sixty or so of us in the room a lifetime's worth of wisdom and knowledge in a weekend. As I reflected on the weekend, I felt there had to be a way to get the wisdom from that room into the hearts and minds of working people everywhere. The desire to spread their experiences and perspectives led to the development of this book.

In 2008 and 2009, the conference was similarly stellar, with all-star lists of speakers who contributed more knowledge and understanding based on years of real life experience in the trenches of the global marketplace. The speakers from those three conferences form the bulk of those whose insights are included in this book.

There are several others who were not present at the conference, but who were asked to submit some of their story as a leader of faith in the global marketplace. It was surprising to me how responsive some of the busiest executives in the world were to our invitation. They took time out of their busy schedules and formulated a contribution for one reason only: so that others could learn how relevant faith is to everything that we do.[1]

And faith is relevant to everything we do, whether we are at church, work, or home! There is a genuine hunger deep in our souls to know that everything we do has purpose and meaning. This is manifest everywhere, whether in a slum in Nairobi or a gathering of high-level executives on Wall Street. Through the years I have noticed that people's questions and search for meaning have centered on certain topics such as calling, stewardship, success, money, etc.

---

1   All of the contributors have graciously foregone any royalties in order that the aggregate total can be donated to the annual Believers in Business Conference.

We have organized the book around these prevalent themes, with the contributors bringing their own insight and experiences to bear on selected issues. This book is not a collection of solutions as much as it is stories and points to consider. The book's purpose is to be immediately practical by stimulating thought and conversation, not by providing simplistic answers to complex topics.

This book can be read cover to cover or in bits and pieces, jumping back and forth. To get the most out of it, talk about what you are reading with other like-minded sojourners, debate with the contributors, and most importantly, apply what you learn because there is nothing better than living a life of faith in Christ everywhere all of the time.

Here's to learning to live our faith in all we do.

CHAPTER ONE
CALLING

"God blessed them and said to them, 'Be fruitful and increase in number; fill the earth and subdue it. Rule over the fish of the sea and the birds of the air and over every living creature that moves on the ground.' "

Genesis 1:28

Calling is a complex and confusing topic for most people. As an ordained minister, I have been introduced on more than one occasion as someone who has a special call from God. While I do think I have a special call from God, I do not view a "special call" as synonymous with ordained ministry, which is the unfortunate implication of the introduction.

In the church, we have been conditioned to accept certain things; one of those is that clergy, church staff, missionaries, and those types of people have callings from God. Frequently this "call" from God takes these people out of the marketplace and into "ministry."

However, I have a long list of friends who say they have been called by God to leave the church and go back to work in the marketplace. Could that possibly be correct? Could God really call people to work in a mundane, "non-ministry-related" job? Isn't a call from God reserved for something more holy and higher than that?

As one who has been a pastor, a missionary, a seminary professor, and an entrepreneur, I can attest that it's all pretty mundane a lot of the time. I have come to believe that my "ministry" is wherever God "calls" me at any point in time. One thing I know for sure is that God calls us to many different places—and that he is calling us *all* to follow him wherever we are.

In the first recorded talk between God and humans, God called human beings to steward the earth's resources. Things have developed since that first conversation and contemporary work, though it certainly does not always reflect God's will and purposes, is still a divinely appointed process through which we fulfill that first calling. Business, far from being a necessary evil, is a vital part of God's mission in the world and is holy ground for those who follow Christ. We just need to recognize it as such.

In this chapter you will read from seasoned executives and business people, who in large part had to develop their own understanding of what is meant by "calling," and through their walk with Christ, have come to realize that business is indeed a worthy call.

DENNIS BAKKE on
THE PURPOSE OF SECULAR WORK (bio p. 251)

What is the purpose of our daily work?

For those of us who are followers of Christ, we know our purpose is to be holy and glorify God. Many of us interpret "glorifying God" as making known his Kingdom and his ways. So how does our workplace fit into such a purpose? Should our workplace be our primary mission field where we seek, through word and deed, to carry out the Great Commission? Is it simply a means to provide for our families and earn enough extra to support our church, missions, and parachurch organizations? Or could it be secular work, even for-profit business, is the principle mission of ministry to which God calls many of us?

I have had the wonderful opportunity over the last twenty-five years to undertake various types of work. Which one do you think was most important to God?
- Nine years coaching youth league football
- The Mustard Seed Foundation—cumulative giving to Christian ministries and scholarships around the world exceeding $80 million
- Ten years as Sunday school teacher, head of missions, and chairman of deacons in our local church

- Twenty years leading a for-profit company (AES Corporation) that served the energy needs of more than 100 million people in thirty-one countries
- Leading a secular nonprofit (Imagine Schools) that operates seventy-three charter schools educating 35,000 students annually—the largest such organization in the nation

Which of these works is most important in God's perspective? Which is most consistent with serving God? Which best served my neighbor as myself?

When I left graduate school for government work in Washington, DC, thirty-nine years ago, my own understanding of work was to earn a living so I could give as much money and time as possible to the church and Christian ministry-related organizations. My high school math teacher exemplified this perspective. In my senior year, she asked me, "Dennis, what are you going to do with your life?" Like any high school senior, I didn't know and gave her the safest answer, "I really don't know, but I am planning to go to college." She had an agenda and replied, "I have some advice for you. Both your older brother, Ray, and your younger brother, Lowel, are committed to be pastors. Someone needs to support them."

She almost perfectly reflected my understanding of the vocational hierarchy available to Christians. The first priority, of course, was to be a missionary to Africa; second, a pastor; third—if you could do neither of those things—you might work for a Christian organization or school; fourth, some kind of service profession such as a doctor, social worker, or advocate. If, however, you weren't spiritual or gifted enough, you could go into business to support those at the top of God's pyramid. While few of us admit to the existence of any such hierarchy, it still seems very much alive in our churches and Christian schools.

Early in the 1980s, my wife and I joined a small group in our local church. One topic we studied was what the Bible said about work and the organizations in which we worked. This was timely for me. I found that God had a very different perspective than what I'd been previously taught. I learned that Genesis tells us God gave us a job even before he gave us a family. We were created in the image of God to be co-creators with him. That's how we glorify him. And that work was to be sublime, joyous, and sacred. Garden work, where we managed or had dominion over creation, was to be our primary mission when the world was still perfect.

What happened in the Garden? Man messed up God's work plan. Sin entered the world and work got harder, but it is not cursed. If anyone thinks work is cursed, they won't have the right attitude. Christ came to redeem work in us. By implication, it seems to me that we who are redeemed are supposed to be co-redeemers of work, to make our ordinary secular work as close as possible to the purposeful, joyous work that God gave us in the Garden, knowing that the redeeming process will not be complete until Christ returns.

Most of the work carried out by biblical heroes was secular:
- Noah was a shipbuilder, a zookeeper, and a cruise-line captain;
- Abraham was a real estate developer;
- Esther was a pageant winner so she could enter a harem before she became a queen;
- Daniel went to Harvard, the King's college, and became president of Iraq.

Most of us are called to secular workplaces, not primarily as evangelists or disciplers, but like these folks in the Bible, our job is to serve the ordinary needs of society as well as our own. Our work is to serve others and along the way our own needs will be met. That's what the great commandment says, "'Love the Lord your God with all your heart, and with all your soul and with all your mind' . . . and . . . 'Love [serve] your neighbor as yourself'" (Matthew 22:37, 39).

Joseph is an Old Testament prototype of Christ. God called Joseph to serve as the Chief Operating Officer of Cairo, Incorporated. In Joseph's secular working role, he probably saved thousands of people from starving to death, only a few of which were family members or followers of Yahweh. He was called to help feed the people, not make them disciples.

What does the New Testament say? Jesus spent eighty-five percent of his working life as a carpenter. The root word for carpenter is *tekton*, which has similar roots to the word "technology." Since there was very little wood in the area, Jesus was probably not a builder of cabinets or other wood products. Research has found the city of Sepphoris was being built around that time, and that Jesus and Joseph likely had jobs as stone masons building homes and other structures for the Greeks and Romans, not necessarily Jewish folks. Jesus probably spent most of his work life as a secular builder in a for-profit business. That is the model most of us should be following.

HOWARD DAHL on
THE SACRED / SECULAR DICHOTOMY (bio pp. 253-254)

When we started Concord in 1977, I wrote my vision for the business. (See Purpose Statement on pages 28-29)

A few points were central to the vision. There was to be no sacred/secular dichotomy. It is important to see all of life as sacred, every detail. My father deeply influenced this viewpoint. He looked at all employees as being of equal value to a company and lived that out in his business practice. There are no small people. We've worked hard to make sure that all of our people are treated as equal members of the company.

Honoring the belief that everyone is of equal value is part of the ongoing conversation I have with our employees. I do a quarterly employee breakfast or lunch where I treat our staff as members of the board of directors. I update them on what's going on in the company, field their questions and listen to their input. Any employee that wants to talk to me personally can. We're small so this is easier to do than in a huge company. We've had a lot of meaningful conversations, and, over the years, many professions of faith.

We also have a lot of employee development programs focused on wellness. Last year, we brought in a nutritional coach to meet with employees individually. It's important to focus on the well-being of our people. If there's one thing that has governed our business, it's the Golden Rule, "Do to others what you would have them do to you."

DAVID MILLER on
THE THEOLOGY OF WORK (bio pp. 260-261)

One of my favorite quotes from Martin Luther King, Jr. is, "If a man is called to be a street sweeper, he should sweep streets even as Michelangelo painted, or Beethoven composed music, or Shakespeare wrote poetry. He should sweep streets so well that all the hosts of heaven and earth will pause to say, 'Here lived a great street sweeper who did his job well.'" It's not necessarily what we do, but how we do it. There are redemptive purposes in knowledge worker jobs, skilled labor, and unskilled labor. A few points about the theology of work:

- **We are co-creators with God.** Think of it as a partnership. Don't forget that God is the managing partner, and we are the junior partners, but we co-create with God. The work is not done.

- **To work is part of humanity.** It is part of human anthropology and the doctrine of humanity. It is part of who we are and what we were created to do. I have yet to see someone who has stopped working, in the paid work sense, and after the first ninety days of playing unlimited golf and tennis, doesn't miss some aspect of the work, if they haven't found new co-creative activities to put their work skills into.

HOWARD DAHL
Purpose Statement
Goals for Concord, Inc.

(1) Defined company purpose.

Too often there exists the sad situation in which people do not mesh their personal life's goals with their vocational activities. There is often a confusion between function and goals resulting in a situation in which people enjoy what they are doing, but are unsure of its connection with their purpose for living. There also exists a common fallacy that one cannot have mixed motives when engaging in business (i.e., altruistic and profit-oriented). A classic case of this would be Rudolph Diesel who designed his famous engine because of a passionate desire to see socio-economic justice. Indeed, a person who has such a dream is far often more highly motivated than one who does not. It is a tragic commentary on the status of much of American free-enterprise that a monolithic raison d'etre seems to be prevalent, viz. money. Be that as it may, Concord, Inc. is being established with some very clear objectives. These objectives are reflective of one person's interpretation of what a Christian's goals should be in the business world.

Personal goals to be reflected in Concord, Inc.

(A) Believing that we are put on this earth not by some sort of cosmic capriciousness, but rather for a purpose ordained by God, it is my desire that Concord might serve as a vehicle to enhance that purpose.

(B) A "successful" life would be one in which the most glory is brought to God. Therefore, one should be continually shrouded with the passion to bring maximum glory to God.

(C) There is no question that there is an immeasurable amount of injustice in the world, and that it brings glory to God wherever justice reigns.

(D) One thought that permeates the whole of Scripture is that God is especially concerned with the plight of the poor, the oppressed, the downtrodden, the "have nots" of this world. A corollary thought is that the "haves" are going to be held especially accountable for what they do in relationship to the "have nots."

(E) There is a great amount of physical, intellectual, and spiritual poverty in much of the Third World.

(F) American Christians have the resources to do something significant to abet the removal of much of this poverty.

G) Concord is thus being established for the purpose of helping to facilitate the growth of the Third World countries; a growth to be reflected intellectually, physically, and spiritually.

(II) Means to accomplish company purpose

The name Concord has been chosen because it reflects the company goals of reaching mutual agreement with the national leadership and farmers in a country before a project is begun.

(A) Development of a farm tractor geared to the subsistence farmer in the Third World.

(B) With the tractor, providing a "comprehensive" agricultural technology package geared toward the present situation in which the farmers find themselves.

(C) Establishment of the Concord Foundation which will receive 10% of the pre-tax profits of Concord, Inc. The money will in turn be given to assist the needy people in their development.

(D) Careful analysis of the markets on a country-by-country basis after which a decision is to be made as to the most strategic method to penetrate each market.

(E) Working in close relationship with Christian missions, foundations, UNIDO, AID, and other relevant organizations.

(F) Involving many individuals in an advisory role who have expertise and share the goals of the company.

(G) Attempt to begin first manufacturing facility overseas..

5-year plan

August 1, 1977-December 31, 1977
Develop 1 prototype by March 1, 1978.
Test prototype between March and August.
January 1, 1978-December 31, 1978
Build 50-100 tractors to be shipped in a comprehensive machinery package to 1 or 2 locations.
January 1, 1979-December 31, 1979
Set up manufacturing facility in Asia, Africa, or Latin America.
Set up CPS type project in one country carefully selected.
January 1, 1980-December 31, 1981
Set up second manufacturing facility and second comprehensive program.

- **There is a time and a season for everything.** (Ecclesiastes) Let us not forget that sometimes work is hard, boring, and monotonous; and sometimes work is easy, joyous, and invigorating. God can be present in both scenarios, if we remember to invite God in. You may be called, for a season, to be in a place that is pretty crummy, and there you are meant to be salt and light for a time. Work honorably and in a God-pleasing way. Hopefully, God will bless you then with a season where work is invigorating and stimulating, where you feel God's creative juices coming out of your fingertips.

- **Sometimes we are rewarded for our work and acknowledged publicly, and other times we are not.** Just as Jesus taught us to pray very privately, and not to show off and brag in front of others, I think we ought to continue to do our work well whether we are rewarded financially and verbally in public or not. Two things matter: both what we do and how we do it. Some jobs are obviously making this creation into a better place, with a more obvious relationship to the coming kingdom of God. In other jobs, it is harder to make that connection. But God can be present in both.

- **Work is both a means and an end to honor God and serve our neighbor.** Work is a form of worshipping God and serving neighbor, pulling together both the vertical and horizontal axis. If we hold this together, we can avoid the extreme of demonizing work on one hand or idolizing it on the other. That's the essence of the Jewish word *Avodah*, and the reason I gave The Avodah Institute that name. The root word for *Avodah* is translated in the Hebrew Scriptures differently, based on the context, it can mean "work," "worship," and "service." Whatever our places and kinds of work may be, our work matters deeply to God. We have a calling right in front of us.

ED MEESE on
OPPORTUNITIES IN THE WORKPLACE (bio pp. 259-260)

I have been in a lot of workplaces in my life. As a matter of fact, I consider it a great asset to have gained a variety of experiences. My wife looks at it a little differently: she says I apparently can't keep a job. Either way, three elements were essential to all of my professional opportunities:

1. Religion and faith have been important elements of every opportunity that I have had. It was God's blessing and God's plan that gave me opportunities to do many different things. With the exception of my first job, I have never had to look for a job. Something always came along, and I had to choose whether to take it or not. I approached each decision with a lot of prayer before choosing to move on to a new job or not.

2. Mentors and leaders have guided me along the way. My first real mentor was a student pastor who was studying for his PhD in the Yale Divinity School while I was an undergraduate. Besides working on his PhD, he was the student pastor for Yale's Lutheran Student Association. It was a great opportunity to learn from him. That was a very important facet of my undergraduate activities at Yale.

3. Reinforced relationships, as I call them, are important to me and will be particularly valuable as you go out into the business world. These are the relationships that encourage us as we work to live according to our beliefs, many of which will be in the workplace.

KEN ELDRED on
THE "CALLING" MYTH (bio p. 254)

When it comes to business as usual, godly traits tend to be overlooked, and nothing seems absolute. Knowledge is increasing at such fantastic rates that we don't have time to learn it all. The world has brought us new thought processes, and because we often don't have time to stop and reflect, we automatically adopt them as our own. So it is with business and common conventions. We buy into them because we hear them over and over again, not because we have seen them proven true.

Churches don't necessarily teach the importance of business from a scriptural perspective, and so we end up operating on conventional wisdom. The idea of myths is not new. In the parable of the talents, the one who buried the talent did so operating under a myth. When the king called the man to account, he replied with a myth about God saying in essence: I knew you were a terrible tyrant reaping where you did not sow. (See Luke 19:20-21.) Myths can ruin your whole understanding of God and what you are called to do. There are a lot of myths that need busting. Here's one:

Committed Christians should go into ministry.

This is a serious issue for people. As a child, my parents dropped me off at church in the morning, and I walked home without going in. It didn't mean a lot to me then. As I grew up, church and the things of God continued to mean very little to me. By the time I got to business school, my whole objective there was to finish, not to reflect on any moral implications. I wasn't even thinking about God. When my wife and I got married, we had no relationship with the Lord whatsoever. After a series of crises in one year, however, God got our attention. We decided to move home to the West Coast. Back home, we thought we should give our children a chance to see what religious life was about, so they could make their own decision.

The plan was to visit my old Presbyterian church, my wife Roberta's Catholic church, and then to move on to various faiths. That should have given them enough to make up their own minds about the religious stuff. Well, we didn't get past my Presbyterian church.

One morning outside the church, I began arguing with God. "I'm not sure if I want to believe in you, and I don't understand what I need to do if I become a Christian. But, I have been listening to the pastor and I am certain if I become a Christian, you will send me off to the mission field first, and that mission field will put me into ministry somewhere, probably in great poverty." I was now five years into my business career, and I had no desire to go off to the mission field. I was in business, and I really wanted to do business. I argued, "Lord, that's not what I want to do." His comment to me was, "So what? What has that got to do with your decision for me?" I finally gave in, "Whatever you decide is okay with me." His response was a verse: "Delight yourself in the Lord and he will give you the desires of your heart" (Psalm 37:4).

My desire was to be in business, so I made a request, "If you want me to be a pastor, then you will need to change the desires of my heart. I trust you, but I need you to do that for me." Not long after, I was waiting for the voice of God to again tell me where he wanted me to go. In the meantime, I was looking at ideas for possibly starting a business. A friend and I had just made a bid to buy a company and were badly beaten out of the deal. Back in my temporary office, he said he had a number of ideas for starting a business. Since I had nothing else to do that day, I encouraged him to lay them out. About halfway down the list of his business ideas, I heard a voice distinctly say, *"That's it."* Immediately I wondered who was speaking? It wasn't my friend. He was in the middle of explaining yet another business idea he had. I sensed it was God talking to me. I stopped my would-be partner and asked him to back up. Dutifully, he began to go through the list again until I said, "That one! Tell me more about that one." God began to work with us.

Our business was to provide computer users in large corporations with all they needed to run their systems. In those days there was no store for that kind of stuff. We focused on putting the concept together. Thirty years ago users bought computer accessories and supplies from the computer manufacturer. We saw an opportunity to by-pass that slow chain of purchasing and provide faster service and lower prices. We decided these sales would be too small to support a sales person, so we were going to build our computer supplies business by direct mail. Up until then, no one had sold anything by direct mail any more complicated than a pencil, let alone rather sophisticated computer-related products. Further, direct mail was considered to be notoriously slow. It was very unusual for a direct mail company to ship everything the same day, which we were going to do. There was no Federal Express. If you ordered something via direct mail, twelve weeks was a good delivery window; eight weeks was pretty good, and six weeks was unbelievable. To get an order to the customer the next day—*nobody* did that! We had decided computer customers wanted fast service and could not wait weeks, let alone days, for a shipment to arrive.

We had little money when we started the company. Daily sales were crucial for us. Since we shipped everything the same day, we had no backlog. Daily sales grew to $1,600, then $1,700, then to over $2,000, then the company sales started to sink. With this growth, we were stretched cash-wise. I was up to my eyeballs financially and began to worry.

I talked to my wife about the sales decline and the doubts I was having about whether I should have even started the company in the first place. Perhaps I had misunderstood God's plan. Perhaps I was supposed to be a missionary after all. My wife's approach to the problem was simple: ask God to show us. Remembering that seven was the biblical number for completeness and perfection, she suggested we pray for a $7,000 day. This was way beyond our best day ever in recorded sales. In fact, it was three times our highest single day's sales, but I agreed. She went further. Since one day could be a coincidence, she believed it would be best to pray for *three* $7,000 days. I thought those numbers were nearly impossible and certainly outrageous. Not wanting to appear unspiritual, I agreed again. We decided to light a candle and keep it burning for ten days while we prayed for three $7,000 days.

We prayed morning and night. For the first five days I was really worried. How could this possibly happen? Sales continued to drift downward. On the fifth or sixth day, I began to feel that if this wasn't where God wanted me. He had something better, and I began to feel hopeful. On the tenth day, which happened to be Sunday night, I got up from the prayer time, and said, "Roberta, I really believe God's going to give us a $7,000 day." There was nothing in the numbers to give me any support, but somehow I knew what God was going to do. And she said, "You know, I feel the same way."

The next morning I went to the office and we had a little business meeting. All four employees showed up. I said, "God is going to give us a $7,000 day today." I wish I had a photograph of the look on their faces! One person's jaw was longer than normal, eyes were larger than normal, and I could practically read their thoughts, *"Where did I put my resumé? The boss has cracked!"*

The day started like any other. Usually incoming telephone orders were constant until about 11:30 a.m., dropping off over lunch, picking up around 2:00 pm and finally tailing off at 4:30 p.m., but this day, sales started about 8:30 in the morning, which was a little unusual. Incoming orders were constant, not overwhelming Nancy, my Customer Service Rep, but very steady—one right after the other.

About 2:00 p.m., Nancy came into my office, "Ken, we could have a $5,000 day today!" She was really excited, and, in her excitement, she was going to let me off the hook. And I said, "No, it's a $7,000 day. That's what we asked for." She looked at me, shook her head, and went away.

At 5:00 p.m. the phones finally stopped ringing with the last call coming from a firm in Hawaii. In those days, as a computer company, we did not actually have a computer. So, we tabulated our daily sales using a ten-key calculator and a piece of paper. We sat there, pretty excited, while Nancy, our sales representative cum accountant, zipped away on the ten-key. She went through the numbers twice, pulled up the total, and put her fingers on the two red numbers at the bottom—$7,000!

I was absolutely over the moon, and called my wife, "Roberta, guess what?" She said, "I know, you had a $7,000 day. Now come home the kids need you." The next two Mondays, we had $7,000 days, then business dropped to $1,900 and then $1,600. But I was the happiest man in town. I didn't really care because I knew that I was right where God wanted me.

Incidentally, we found that our sales did drop only to come on stronger as the year unfolded in later months. These $7,000 days stood out in our statistics as three very unusual beacons or spikes on the daily sales chart. These spikes were never repeated although the company grew to roughly $400 million in sales per year.

Pastors are not the only serious Christians. Serious Christians are those who commit their lives to God whether in the ministry or at work. That has been my experience, and I pray that it is yours. Don't ever let people say that there is a division between us or that one person's work is nobler than another's. I defy you to find one reference in Scripture that supports the idea that God is not interested in the work of business folks or that pastors are somehow closer to God because of their clerical vocation. Work in the secular world is just as important to God as being a pastor.

BONNIE WURZBACHER on
BUSINESS AS A CALLING (bio p. 268)

For over twenty-five years I have worked for The Coca-Cola Company and am currently Senior Vice President of Global Customer Leadership. Paradoxically, my loving and faithful Christian parents, now deceased, would have been so disappointed in my career choice—at least initially. However, I don't think they would be now. Allow me to explain.

As a young girl growing up in the Midwest, I was clearly drawn to business. Whether it was erecting lemonade stands, organizing and marketing neighborhood puppet shows or dog walking services, entrepreneurship came naturally. I was good at it and enjoyed it, but had few, if any, role models in business and never really considered it as a career, much less a calling.

Thankfully, in my formative years, reverence and service to God and his Kingdom was lovingly ingrained in me by my family. I descend from a long and unbroken line of dedicated pastors, missionaries, doctors, and teachers. Following in the steps of my parents and grandparents, I was blessed to be educated at Wheaton College surrounded by many kindred "PKs" (pastors' kids) and "MKs" (missionaries' kids). The idea that one could serve God through a business career was inconceivable to me—and to my family.

Graduating from Wheaton with a degree in education, I immediately embarked on a career in service as an elementary school teacher in an economically disadvantaged community. The rewards of that work were increasingly dimmed by the absence of a meritocracy, the tyranny of tenure in the public school system, and the frustrating indifference of many of the students' parents.

My search for a new career led me to a sales opportunity in the hospitality industry and shortly thereafter to Coca-Cola. Gradually, during that journey, I've come to learn that all believers are called to be in "full-time Christian work," not just those in religious-oriented vocations. Indeed, I've studied, pondered, and received inspired mentoring on the meaning and aspects of a "calling" and how God can be glorified—and his Kingdom advanced—through our daily work.

BONNIE and STEVE WURZBACHER on FRUITFUL WORK AS BOTH A BLESSING and EXPECTATION OF GOD (bios on pp. 268 & 269, respectively)

There are only two resources available to us for fulfilling God's requirements:
1)   the natural resources he has placed on the earth, and

2)   the "intellectual capital" he has gifted to each of us.

God's original purpose for us was twofold:

1)   to "Be fruitful and multiply," (Genesis 1:28 ESV), i.e., to develop the social world—to build families, churches, schools, cities, and the like.

2)   to "fill the earth and subdue it" (Genesis 1:28 ESV), i.e., harness the natural world—plant crops, construct buildings, invent, innovate, compose, and the like.

I believe he has called us to create God-honoring cultures and civilizations.

We continue God's own creative work in this world by harnessing the power and developing the potential that God originally built into his creation. We are each called to be his representatives and stewards in this world, reflecting his holy and loving care for it.

We don't get meaning *from* our work;
we must bring meaning *to* our work.

God needs his people in boardrooms and business offices, just as much as he does in churches, classrooms, and operating rooms.

Certainly there have been high profile disappointments in the business world recently. Enron, Adelphia, and other failed corporations remind us of our flawed condition and the potential for harm, yet they also create a compelling case for the need of Christian ethics in business—and believers who understand how to glorify God in both the product and the process of their work.

Many Christians, seriously committed to their faith, struggle with the divide imposed by modern society between the sacred and secular spheres—our work being strictly imprisoned in the secular. God needs his people everywhere. All vocations, the business world included, can be practiced in ways that honor the

Lord and use our talents to serve him. Scripture commands us to be sent "into *the world*," yet not be "of *the world*" (John 17:18, 16, emphasis mine).

DAVID MILLER on THE HUNGER FOR DISCUSSION of FAITH IN BUSINESS (bio pp. 260-261)

It is fascinating that the corporate world is increasingly interested in faith at work. About twenty years ago when I was starting my career with IBM, if someone had asked me what I did last weekend, and I replied, "Wow! I heard a great sermon at church!" everyone would have run away and thought I was a religious zealot. But today when I go to a cocktail party in New York City, attend an event in Zurich, or travel anywhere in the world and am asked, "What line of work are you in?" I often say, somewhat mischievously, "Well, I'm in the God business." Inevitably, that's followed by silence. Then questioners ask, "What do you mean?" I tell them, "I used to be a partner at an investment bank, but now I think about God and the roles God and theology have in our daily work lives." Usually there's a little bit more silence, then one of two reactions: Either they quickly abandon me to grab a drink at the bar, or they start a conversation that often lasts the whole evening. The fascinating thing is eight out of ten people don't run to the bar. They say, "Can I talk to you?"

People are trying to connect the dots between Sunday and Monday, or Saturday and Monday, based on what their Sabbath day is. And they're trying to find other people who want to talk about that "work-worship gap." There is a hunger for it among the different generations. The mere fact that Yale University recruited me to help establish, lead, and serve as executive director of the university's Center for Faith & Culture, that people are reading my book *God at Work* and bringing me in to give talks and consultations around the country, and that Princeton University appointed me to its faculty to continue and expand that work, launching its new Faith & Work Initiative, are all extraordinary. These things would not have happened a few years ago.

I've done a lot of work with my friend John Tyson, the chairman of Tyson Foods, on how to become a faith-friendly company, which is different from a faith-based company. John recently gave the University of Arkansas significant endowment funding for a new center, which is called the John Tyson Faith and Spirituality in the Workplace Center. That business leaders like John Tyson would see the importance of faith at work, and that a public university would accept such a gift, is extraordinary. This "Faith at Work" movement is a movement, and it has gained intellectual and practical credibility.

Here's another example of the interest in overcoming the Work-Worship Gap. One of the prominent large Swiss banks invited me to give a talk on business ethics to a German-speaking group of successful businesswomen in a castle outside of Zurich, Switzerland. The group consisted of high net-worth individuals who were either business owners, heirs to great wealth, or senior executives who had made a lot of money. Half of the women were clients and the other half prospective clients. It was one of those gentle, low-key kinds of marketing events, and I was asked to talk about ethics in business. One of my Power-Point slides simply asked: "What is the source of your ethics?" I commented that the minute you open up the question of source, inevitably issues of the transcendent, the metaphysical, and God comes into play. I mentioned that most people's ethics are shaped by a variety of factors including parents, relatives, teachers, coaches, spiritual leaders, culture, upbringing, and traditions. Then I moved the conversation on to another topic. But guess what? During dinner, cocktail hour, and until about 2:00 a.m., I ended up talking with and answering questions from several conference attendees about God and Jesus. It was extraordinary. Of course, the setting was safe and the tone was one of respect and desire for personal growth.

DAVID MILLER on THE RELEVANCE
OF FAITH in THE MARKETPLACE (bio pp. 260-261)

Once a month I lead a group in Greenwich, Connecticut, called the Greenwich Leadership Forum, or GLF. It was founded about five years ago by a few people, including Russell Reynolds, the founder of the prominent executive search firm of the same name. Russ and a few friends knew that Greenwich, the hedge fund capital of the world, is one of the wealthiest zip codes in the country. They thought if they could get people in Greenwich to care more about faith than golf, it could make a difference in the marketplace. When Russ and his friends asked me to set up a program around that, I declined because I'm not a big fan of programs. Eventually I agreed to set up a three-part pilot to see if people would be interested. I said, "If people come, fine, we will turn it into something, but let's not presume an outcome."

We decided to hold the meetings at 6:30 a.m. at the Indian Harbor Yacht Club. I nixed the idea of holding it at a church to avoid repelling people who aren't interested in church. I thought twelve or fifteen people might show up. Yet, in this supposedly spiritually arid place called Greenwich, the event produced thirty people. Astounding. We now have average attendance of over one hundred people per session, and over eight hundred people on our mailing list. Half of the time I invite CEOs and interview them doing my Oprah imitation. We talk about how they connect the dots between faith and work, how they deal with failure, temptation, struggle, and the plurality of worldviews. Other times, I teach from some story out of the previous week's *The Wall Street Journal.* We discuss whether there are resources in the Christian faith and explore teachings that offer a different perspective and worldview. GLF approaches these questions out of the Christian tradition, but people from any and no tradition are welcome to participate.

I always ask at the beginning of a session, "Who is here for the first time?" and invariably there are several newcomers who were invited by friends. It is all spread by word of mouth. I explain that the Greenwich Leadership Forum is about answering this question: "What does the Bible, which everyone tries to follow on Sunday, have to do with the *Wall Street Journal* and Monday through Friday work life?" I hold a copy of the Bible in one hand and the *Wall Street Journal* in the other. For many people, the answer is "nothing." They see themselves operating in two different worlds. But I argue just the opposite: your Sunday church world has everything to do with your rest-of-the-week world. If you read the Bible through the lens of the marketplace, you'll be blown away by how much both testaments—the old Hebrew Scriptures and the New Testament—have to say about your behavior in and attitude toward the marketplace and money. Jesus talked about money all the time—and not always in condemnatory tones. *The Wall Street Journal* does not need to be your marketplace bible; rather, God's Bible ought to be where you seek guidance for marketplace parameters.

I would be selling you a bill of goods if I tried to say that the Bible was an easy how-to manual. It doesn't say to just do steps one, two, three, and you'll be rich and successful. It is a rich, textured, and living set of stories about the human condition, where wisdom oozes from almost every page. Both testaments are filled with inspiring stories of great men and women and many fallen heroes. Integrating faith and work can be a struggle; but the Bible contains all of the wisdom and the strength you need to recover from failure, prevent it in the future, and lead a life that is pleasing to God.

If you would have told me a few years ago that I would be standing in front of audiences around the world talking about God, faith and work, I would have said you were smoking something illegal. That wasn't me. That wasn't how I grew up. The Sunday mornings of my youth in New Jersey began with my devout, Methodist mother taking my older brother and me off to Sunday School while my genius father, who was a PhD research scientist for RCA, sat at home in his recliner chair listening to loud classical music and reading the Sunday *The New York Times* cover to cover. He had no time for organized religion. It intellectually was not up to snuff for him. He posed lots of hard questions: What about other religions? What about evil? What about illness? What about war? What about pestilence? Because he couldn't answer them, he assumed that the proposition of God was false.

As a kid, I was always asking myself: Who is right? Mom or Dad? In a way, it turns out they were both right: My dad was right to ask these hard questions, but he came to the wrong conclusions; and my mom was right to take Christianity at face value with a pure, child-like faith. If only we all had the faith of a child, even as we wrestle with life's toughest questions, the world might be a better place.

As I grew up, my "life question" revolved around blind faith versus intellectual discovery, the sacred versus the secular. As I got older, I reframed that question as: "What does my faith have to do with my work? Is faith just something I compartmentalize? Is it just a Sunday proposition?" If I really took my faith seriously and believed that God exists, and Jesus is who he said he is, then ought not my approach to work and leadership be different? Faith ought to impact everything I do Monday through Friday, not just when I have my Sabbath time.

After eight terrific and exciting years at IBM, I accepted a position in London as managing director of State Street Bank and Trust, and later went to work at Midland Bank PLC as part of its turnaround team for the securities service business. HSBC acquired Midland, and I stayed on to run HSBC's global custody and securities business. Finally, during the last couple of years that I worked in London, I was a partner in a small, private merchant banking firm doing cross-border mergers. Since I spoke German, my focus was the securities industry and our acquisitions in German-speaking countries. It was during this time that I gradually discerned a calling to study theology.

I wish I could tell you it was some dramatic event or life crisis that drove me to study the mystery of God. Truth be told, I loved my wife, I loved my job, I was making more money than I knew what to do with, and I was satisfied and fulfilled. Nevertheless, I discerned this tugging, this sort of whisper to study theology. After about eighteen months of discernment and some fits and starts, I finally concluded that, for whatever crazy reason, God was calling me to study theology. So, at the partners meeting when it came time to discuss new business, I raised my hand and said, "I have discerned this calling to go study theology." There was dead silence. You could have heard a pin drop. Jaws did drop. One of my partners said, "You think you've received a calling from God?" "Yes," I replied, deeply embarrassed. Without skipping a beat, he said, "Hasn't God ever heard of call-waiting?"

DAVID MILLER on
CONNECTING FAITH and WORK (bio pp. 260-261)

Soon after that my wife Karen, a highly successful lawyer turned law professor, and I returned to the States. I studied for several years in seminary, first for an MDiv and then a PhD in social ethics. As you've gathered by now, my passion is connecting faith and work. My personal mission statement is: How do we integrate the claims of our faith with the demands of our work? We work in a world and in a workplace that make demands on us that aren't always aligned with the claims of the Gospel. The code of ethics on Wall Street is different from the code of ethics in the Bible. How do we integrate the claims of our faith with the demands of our work?

My friend Bob Buford wrote a *New York Times* best-seller entitled, *Halftime: Changing Your Game Plan from Success to Significance*. Now theologically, what is wrong with that title? Bob made a bundle of money with cable TV in Texas. In mid-life he experienced a tragedy and some profound, life-changing events. Since then, he has dedicated the second half of his life to strategic philanthropy and a lot of other extraordinary things. He's a super guy.

His thesis in *Halftime* is once you have made your bundle, you should cash in, step out of the business world where you made your wealth and start finding significance in your life by getting involved in good works and noble projects. The problem I have with that thesis is what about the first half of your life? Does that count for nothing other than to make money for later "giving back"?

In response, one of the books I am writing has the working title of *Full Time: Finding Significance in your Success*. I believe your whole work life, whether you are an analyst, an engineer, a secretary, or a CEO, is full-time and significant. We err if we think that work can only be a calling and fulfilling if it is really stimulating, or if we work only in order to later be a philanthropist. Look at the biblical stories on calling. In most of those narratives, people were called to things that were not fun, glorious, or glamorous. They were not called to things you would aspire to do. Callings can be tough, just like the workplace. Let's embrace that and find God in the daily, the mundane, and the profane.

For example, God says to Moses, a convicted felon on the run: "I want you to pop back in and visit Pharaoh and tell him to free all the slaves." That was not a pleasant calling.

Often we start our careers working those ludicrously long hours and doing meaningless tasks, or so they seem, as we develop our professional competence. That is the place for us to be the face of Christ. That is when we are tested, learn where the ethical boundaries are, learn how to say "no," when to say "yes," and perhaps how to suffer the consequences. Those are trying times but can also be times of calling. They equip us for later things that might seem bigger or more meaningful. It is in the trenches where a lot of the learning action is.

I do a lot of one-on-one consulting, counseling, coaching, and advising with CEOs and senior executives. Many of them will start the one-on-one relationship by saying, "Aw, Miller, I really envy you. You are in full-time Christian work." And I reply, "Do you mind if I ask you a question? Are you baptized?" Most of them are. I continue, "Well, according to what I read in the Bible, you are in full-time Christian work, too!" Being a research analyst is full-time Christian work. So is being a ditch digger, or a CEO. It is all about where we are planted, and being faithful to your call there and beyond.

Now to be fair, in some fields it is a lot harder to make the connection between work and doing what is God-pleasing and honorable. There probably are some fields that people of faith ultimately should say, "That is just too toxic, too evil, too wrong, too bad, too much against my principles. I should not work in that environment." But in general, I tend to stretch the boundary of where Christians ought to work. A Christian ought to work in as dangerous a place as possible, so long as you can protect yourself. If you don't like how certain industries operate, get in them and try to change them. Maybe you'll be there just for a season. Maybe you'll work there for just a few years. It could be very difficult for you spiritually or ethically, but maybe you will begin to create change. You can protect, empower, and encourage others. You can make a difference.

Dietrich Bonheoffer, the Lutheran pastor, ethicist, and martyr who got involved in overthrowing Hitler, is my favorite theologian. He said, to paraphrase, "It is better to get your hands dirty in order to try to prevent evil and then to fall on the mercy of God for forgiveness then it is to sit on the sidelines and be proud of your clean hands." That motivates me.

what's your calling?

join the conversation at
www.oursoulsatwork.com/calling

CHAPTER TWO
LEADERSHIP

"The Son of Man did not come to be served, but to serve."
Matthew 20:28

Through the years, as a participant, consultant, and researcher in a variety of organizations, I have come to believe that nothing is more paramount to the success, health, and well-being of an organization than who its leaders are. It begins and ends with leadership.

For my doctoral dissertation, I researched twelve businesses and learned a lot about the interconnectedness of business organizations. The direct correlation between leadership attitudes and practices and the health of the business was astonishing. If a leader was wise and humble, then it was often reflected in the organization. If the leader was negative and arrogant, then that was found throughout the business as well.

The Bible talks a great deal about how we are to treat one another. For leaders, these teachings are magnified because leaders, by definition, are people who have influence over others. The actions of leaders affect people in ways that leaders frequently fail to recognize.

Everyone is a leader to some degree. Picking up and reading this book is an indication that you are more inclined to leadership than perhaps many others are. Whether you are a seasoned leader or an emerging one, we can all learn from one another.

In this chapter, we have the opportunity to learn from some remarkable leaders who have unique thoughts on what it means to be simultaneously a follower of Christ and a leader of people in the global marketplace.

DENNIS BAKKE on
THE MOST FUN WORKPLACE in HUMAN HISTORY (bio p. 251)

My great desire is to create the most fun workplace in human history.

On one of my very first trips to our first operating power plant just outside of Pittsburgh, the plant manager took me on a quick tour. On the tour I was unable to see everything in detail as I would have liked. As a result, I returned to the plant after my board meetings at a local college around 11:00 in the evening, and found myself staying until 3:00 or 4:00 in the morning talking to the staff who worked the late shift. One conversation in particular struck me deeply and forever changed how I would look at the workplace.

I was told that the people who come to work in my company at twenty-two or twenty-three years old would circle a date on the calendar thirty-five years in the future indicating when they could "get out." My workplace was like a jail sentence. It was a good workplace, but you don't circle a time thirty-five years in the future when you'll finally "get out" if you think the place is a fun place to work. It bothered me.

I talked to folks about why working at my company would feel like a jail sentence, but it wasn't till I started hearing about their life away from work that I understood. When they talked about their "outside" life, their whole demeanor changed. They loved things like bowling and golf and hunting. This gave me an idea. What is it that makes the things they were talking about fun? Take basketball, for example. What's the fun thing about playing basketball? Making a basket! When is the most fun time to make a basket? When the basket breaks the tie in the championship game. There isn't one of us who doesn't dream of ourselves in a similar situation sometime. Why is that so special? We're made in the image of God, and God wants us to use our gifts and talents to make something wonderful happen. We want to be the one to make a difference—especially when it matters most.

In the workplace, decision-making is what allows us to "make something happen."

A McDonald's ad featuring Michael Jordan noted he had forty-six chances in his career to make the last tie-breaking shot. He says, "I missed more than I made." Still, he loved basketball. It's not necessarily about winning. It's about being put in the decision-making position—being responsible for a particular outcome.

The essence of humanness is that we can think, reason, make a decision, and then hold ourselves accountable for the results. When we get the chance to do that, when we get to try for the shot, even if we don't win, it's the best experience ever.

As I reflected on this discovery, it changed my entire concept of how business should work in regards to decision making. It turned my view upside down. Now, I try to limit myself to one decision a year, and let others make the majority of decisions. We require decision-makers to get advice first, but the decision is ultimately theirs.

We are made in the image of God as individuals, but are put in families and companies to work. This is the essence of a joyful workplace. It's not how much you pay or how nice you are to employees or how long their vacations are that makes a place fun. It's how much they get to walk out being made in the image of God—to what extent they are able to make decisions and take responsibility.

The Bible is gives us two great job descriptions:
1)   The Genesis stewardship mission, co-creating and co-managing
        with God (Genesis 1).
2)   The "Great Commission" to make disciples (Matthew 28).

I believe businesses are supposed to be part of the stewardship mission.

The purpose of business is not primarily to make money. In this modern age,

God likes to use people involved in business for carrying out the great commandment to love and serve our neighbors as ourselves.

Jesus' parable of the talents is my favorite work story in the Bible (Matthew 25:14-30). The master/boss sends employees out to work. He encourages them to take risks, make decisions, and undertake random acts of responsibility. The boss never makes any of the decisions about their work, never approves their projects. The only person who gets in trouble is the one who gets tangled up in risk management. Those that invested wisely and aggressively risked the most. It's similar to Genesis where God turns over management of the earth to Adam and to his heirs (us), and even gives away the most important decision of a person's life—to choose or reject God. In the parable of the talents, the boss ends with "Enter into the joy of your master" (Matthew 25:21, 23 ESV). There's joy in working as God meant us to.

In Kazakhstan we took over a power plant; one of the largest in the world. Our plant manager from Hawaii came with me to look at the plant. There were supposedly 5,000 people assigned to work in the power plant (although I doubt more than 3,000 ever worked there). I tried to get them to understand that we were about letting people make decisions. There was absolutely no response, just blank stares. They could not relate. They were not used to acting or being treated like people.

So, I left my Hawaiian manager there to lead the people and went back every summer. On my last trip there, three years later, I asked them to tell me stories. They told how their lives had been changed. They were able to make decisions, things happened, and sometimes things didn't work out, but they had a purpose for living. At the end of the session there was a five- to ten-minute standing ovation—a celebration of pure joy.

It is not optional to give people freedom to make decisions, nor is it optional for leaders who are followers of Christ to refrain from making decisions. It is necessary for the fulfillment of the stewardship commission.

Labor and *opus* are two Latin words for "work." *Labor* conjures up a picture of something hard and difficult. *Opus* denotes something creative and wonderful. When you do the *work* God has called you to do, do it with a passion, joy, and the love befitting God's call on your life.

HOWARD DAHL on
THE CALL OF LEADERSHIP (bio pp. 253-254)

Being a leader begins with seeing yourself as called to a position of leadership and therefore to service. "If you want to be great, you must be the servant of all the others " (Matthew 20:26 CEV). A lot of us want to be called a servant, but we don't want to be treated as one. It can be difficult to have humility about your call and your role when you've had success and lots of positive feedback. Part of the call of leadership is to take the well-being of all of your employees seriously—to see your position as a steward charged to care for your employees.

DAVID MORKEN on FOLLOWING
CHRIST'S EXAMPLE OF LEADERSHIP (bio pp. 261-262)

Most of our 170 employees work in our three-story building in Cary, North Carolina. It's hugely humbling to lead such a large and talented team. Christ's life demonstrates principles that inform leadership every hour and every minute, and his example of leadership begins with serving.

I'm not deceived about myself. I know I am very mortal and can make many, many mistakes. To be in a position to hire someone is humbling and to be in a position to fire them is also humbling. Christ's example of humility is mind-blowing. He was the greatest man to ever walk the planet and was a servant, washing the feet of others, giving his life, taking on sin he didn't deserve. With him as my Savior, it's incumbent upon me to make sure I don't have an elitist approach to leadership.

There is great value in hierarchy, chain of command, and authority; without those, people usually do not accomplish what they're most capable of accomplishing. However, how you handle authority and how you treat people is key. You can easily crush somebody's spirit by demeaning them, not believing in them, exalting yourself and taking credit for their work, or, even worse, by trying to do *their* job from a position above them. Keeping Christ's example in mind reminds me I am here to serve.

DENNIS BAKKE on
INFLUENCING LEADERS (bio p. 251)

If you are not a leader now, you are likely going to be a leader someday. Understanding the role of leadership now prepares you for the future. You also have a chance to teach those leading with you the biblical way to lead.

Warning: You may get fired. I was at the World Bank teaching about changing the way we do things. Located in Washington, DC, the World Bank is involved in microfinance and other financial assistance around the globe. About 10,000 people work for the bank and 8,000 are housed in Washington. A young woman, a middle manager for Bolivia, asked how she could implement the changes I was suggesting. I told her, "You can do all of these things, but you and the people who work for you need to move to Bolivia. Give your people the freedom to make decisions after getting advice from you and their colleagues. You will have to protect your people from the bosses above you. Also you're probably going to lose your job. If you're not prepared to lose your job, you probably won't have the courage to make the changes."

She responded by moving her team to Bolivia and creating a successful team. It was hard work and she had to run interference with her bosses to let her people make decisions. You have to free your subordinates to make decisions, but you also have to protect them from senior management who don't see the importance of this kind of empowerment. It's difficult, but not impossible, to do your part as a leader from a "lower" position.

HARRI SUNDVIK with
VARIOUS LESSONS FOR LEADERS (bio p. 267)

Lesson 1: Accountability

Recently, an investment bank board chairman asked a president, "How can you lose billions? Risk management is in your job description, and we pay you millions of dollars. How can it be that you didn't know?" He replied, "It didn't go under my nose," meaning it wasn't under his direct supervision, so how could he be held responsible for it.

What is that? It suggests there is no accountability. There are two sides to this: the business level and personal level. Make sure you have somebody in your life bold enough, in the business context or a personal friend, to speak into your life, to bring things to your attention when they are out of whack. Things happen quickly, and, without accountability, you simply become part of it.

Lesson 2: Transparency and trust

One weekend during the financial crisis, some Wall Street bankers got together and on Monday came out with a brilliant idea. They would put all the bad assets together in a superfund—*problem solved!* This superfund idea was alive for six weeks, lots of lawyers and accountants did fantastic work to make it happen, but it didn't come to be. Warren Buffet killed it saying, "You need to print third party equity if you create this superfund." He was saying you must have a third party looking into the quality of those assets, or it's going to be an even bigger mess. He was asking for transparency. The superfund did not pass the transparency test.

Lesson 3: Substance over form

Accountants think about this rule probably ten times a day. Over the course of your professional life, things will come across your desk that look absolutely fantastic. Lots of smart people have been doing work on an investment, a memorandum, a prospectus, or whatever. From the outside it looks perfect and real, but when you start looking deeper it is not what it first appeared. When you are responsible, don't get confused by the fact that something looks as though it's been done by the rules. Dig deeper; especially before making an executive decision.

I often work with CEOs in the mergers and acquisitions context. It's fascinating. We may have a transaction ready to be signed Monday, and the last minute on Friday the CEO begins sending some very specific questions about some very important things. Other times, a CEO is not so focused on details and feels as if the form and process has been followed and so everything should be okay. Don't get taken by the form, but take time to look into the substance.

The bottom line is this: *If something looks too good to be true, it probably is.* I've seen this many, many times. One evening, there was a man next to me at our annual dinner. He had quickly made millions. A year later, we found out his finances were not what they appeared to be. There are situations when you need to take a bold step and talk about these things openly, ask the probing questions, and be willing to take what can be an awkward and difficult stance. We see many market-driven situations where things are going well for a long time, but we really need to make sure what is behind it before we jump on board with it.

JOHN TYSON on
FAITH IN LEADERSHIP (bio pp. 267-268)

Faith helps me tremendously in the marketplace. In day-to-day business problems, it helps me see the impact I have on the individuals I'm dealing with. Also my faith enables me to let things go.

In leadership positions, we get on a treadmill, and every time we think we are in shape, they turn the treadmill up again. My faith allows me to slow down and realize the broader issue. One day, they'll turn that treadmill off, and if we don't have our faith in place, we're going to fall flat on our face and be lost. We will have been chasing the treadmill of life—the next bonus, the next job promotion, or whatever—and find ourselves asking, "What do I do now?" because we've missed something essential.

Most of all, my faith allows me to step back and acknowledge that all of us are just trying to get up and get along every day—to make a difference and find the right answers. Some days are better than others, but, in the end, we're striving to honor God. We'll get it eighty percent right. We'll never get one hundred percent right one hundred percent of the time, but eighty percent is not bad in the business world.

STEVE REINEMUND on
LEADERS SHARING FAITH in THE WORKPLACE (bio p. 264)

The higher we go in an organization, particularly in a publicly held company, the more sensitive we must be to not create a situation or the perception that in order to advance one must embody the same beliefs as the leadership. Some may disagree with this perspective, and I respect that, but personally, I am careful how overtly I express my faith. I do not want people to feel they can't succeed if they believe differently than I do. They must embrace the same general values and ethics, but their path to acquiring these can be very different.

I have not taken an active role in trying to evangelize, especially in the workplace. The success of leaders is based on their principles. You can derive those principles in many ways. For me, they come through my faith, but I respect however you arrive at those principles as long as you have the same high ethical standards as the company. And I leave it at that. In public and even in private companies, leaders have to be sensitive to not project their faith onto others.

ED MEESE on
DECISION MAKING (bio pp. 259-260)

Probably the most difficult job of any leader, whether in business or government or education, is making decisions. That's when prayer is particularly important. The two areas that I find the most difficult are firing people and killing people. The only things that can help you through firing employees are: first, work hard in deciding that this is the right solution in a particular situation; second, pray about how to do it; and, third, help the person who has to be fired leave in a dignified way and move on to the next phase of their career.

The other issue, the death penalty, was also difficult for me and required a lot of prayer. I had two jobs in which I had to make those decisions. The first was as a prosecutor in the District Attorney's Office in Alameda County, during which time I had to decide what the penalty should be. The second was as the Governor's Legal Affairs Secretary—my first job in Sacramento. I had to determine clemency recommendations to the governor in death penalty cases. Around 1968, we had three death penalty cases before us. The governor had three choices for each case: He could permit the execution to go forward; he could commute the sentence to something less than death, or he could order a temporary suspension while more information was gathered. As it turned out, the governor picked a different path for each of the three cases. In one case, a person with a very long criminal record committed a very serious homicide, killing two police officers as he was trying to escape from a robbery. I recommended to the governor—and he concurred—that the execution be carried out. The second case had to do with a man who had committed a heinous crime, throwing a firebomb into his girlfriend's apartment, killing two of her children. There was enough evidence, in my opinion, to show he suffered from some mental illness. I recommended that the Governor commute that sentence. In the third case, we asked for more time to investigate, and it was at that time that the Supreme Court in California suspended all death penalty cases. Those were wrenching experiences, but prayer helped tremendously, as did the opportunity to talk these matters over frankly with Governor Reagan and come to conclusions that we both were satisfied with.

I have been extremely lucky in my life. I can't explain why things happened to me other than it was God's providence. I am very grateful for that. I share my experiences with you because they show how fruitful it is to have God in our lives and how much he helps us in our daily routines, let alone in our very tough situations.

DENNIS BAKKE on
DELEGATING DECISIONS (bio p. 251)

The "choose me" test is the first step in identifying folks who are ready to make decisions. Picture children on the school ground choosing teams. Everyone is shouting, "Choose me." Very early, we adopted "choose me" as an indicator of who was ready. They needed to be saying, "I want to do that. I want to take the risk of making decisions and being a leader." Some are not ready, and we give them more time. Usually the biggest problem is that folks want to run off without getting advice.

Most adults want to make decisions. God created every one of us with the ability and even a need to make decisions. It's the way God intended it to be.

ED MEESE on
DEALING WITH THE MEDIA (bio pp. 259-260)

Of all the things you have to deal with in public life, dealing with the press is one of the toughest. The press is not there to write flattering stories about people. As the commentators say facetiously, "If they bleed, it leads." During my career, both in Sacramento and in Washington, DC, most news people had very different political philosophies than I did, Governor Reagan did, or President Reagan did. So it was very tough. The only thing you can do is be honest. Always tell the truth, stand your ground, be very candid, but also be very firm with members of the press.

I had an interesting experience during my first month as Attorney General. Years earlier someone had decided to place the Justice Department pressroom just outside the door of the Attorney General's office. Journalists would literally hang around outside the doorway trying to see who was coming in to meet with the Attorney General and who wasn't. This did not make for a very productive relationship because the journalists would often misinterpret why certain people were coming in and others weren't. Since we needed the room for the Office of Legal Policy, we moved the pressroom down to the first floor. The press was very upset. The day we moved them, several reporters boycotted a lunch I was scheduled to have with them. I told the press, "Actually, you are going to have more access to me because I don't go through the main door to my office. I have an elevator that goes directly through to the basement. With your pressroom on the first floor, I will be available to you any time and every time I walk by your offices. I will come in and, if you want to talk, I will talk." I, in fact, did that, and they did have more direct access to me than before. Eventually, they got over it all and started coming to lunch again.

how does Christ affect your leadership?

join the conversation at
www.oursoulsatwork.com/leadership

CHAPTER THREE
CHARACTER

"May your whole spirit, soul and body be kept blameless at the coming of our Lord Jesus Christ."

1 Thessalonians 5:23b

Followers of Christ generally understand that we are called to live according to his teachings and example. Yet it is frequently difficult to know how that translates into our work lives in ways other than, say, "Don't lie, cheat, or steal." We know there are a few things we should not do. So we avoid those, do our work, and go our merry way.

However, character is a much deeper issue than simply avoiding a few obvious wrongs. It is also about what we do and how we live. Our character is, perhaps, most clearly revealed when times are the toughest. Many businesses are going through very tough times financially right now; some are even collapsing. As a result, our collective character is being challenged. How we handle the trying circumstances of our lives shapes and forms who we are.

Character is exposed in both the best of times and the worst of times. It can be seen in how we treat others. Character is who we are at our core. As people of faith in the global marketplace, we are called to live as Christ, regardless of our situation. This means to conduct ourselves with integrity in times of adversity, to treat people with kindness and respect, and a host of other things that are easier said than done.

Life at work is not as it is at church where we can get by with smiling, greeting one another, and saying we're fine. In the workplace we spend endless hours with one another trying to work out difficult situations, and as pressures mount, both our good and bad sides are revealed. In this chapter, we learn from leaders who have developed strong character through a variety of life circumstances.

HOWARD DAHL on
INTEGRITY (bio pp. 253-254)

Integrity includes never asking any employee to do something that compromises his or her own ethics. For example, never ask a salesman to exaggerate or to deceive in any way to get a sale. Never allow yourself or employees to speak ill of competitors.

There was a time in our company's history when we got into deep financial difficulty. Our bank called in our line of credit and we owed two hundred thirty people money. Our bank wanted us to go into bankruptcy. It was November 20, 1987, almost at the end of the farm crisis of the 1980s. I prayed and fasted for about sixty hours, and out of that came a letter that I wrote to all 230 of our suppliers.

In thinking through what to do, the clarity that I discovered was unbelievable. How would I want to be treated if I were owed money? The answer was that I would want the truth, the whole truth. So I wrote a letter spelling out all the ugly details of where we were financially. Over the next two years, I communicated with our creditors through a series of letters and personally took the accounts payable calls. I didn't want any of our employees to receive abuse from people to whom we owed money. After two years, we were able to work through it and pay them all back. We received incredible feedback from those people we had owed money to. There was only one company out of 230 that moved against us and tried to sue us to force collection. The rest were gracious and thanked me for being straightforward with them.

One of the key issues of business success in any situation is authentic transparency.

Mr. Dahl's letters are located in the Appendix.

DAVID MILLER on AUTHENTICITY
in FAITH-FRIENDLY INITIATIVES (bio pp. 260-261)

I got to know one of the Jewish employees at one of the Tyson Foods Midwestern plants. While researching the idea of allowing people to express their faith more at work, I tried out the language of being "faith friendly" on him. When I asked him what he thought, he responded, "Frankly, I'm relieved." I asked, "Why?" He explained, "You've given me ground to stand on. I no longer have to slip out on Friday if I want to go off to Shabbat and be embarrassed while everyone else is off to a bar or something. I now have infrastructural support as a member of a minority religion in this company." Then he offered some helpful advice: "Make sure that this doesn't just become a Trojan horse for shoving something down people's throat: it has to be truly authentic. If this plays out like Johnny (Tyson) intends, I'm very, very excited about it."

COREY BELL on
RESPECT AND KINDNESS (bio p. 251)

I try to respect every single person, every single day. We can disagree about business, about faith, about other things in life, but that doesn't mean I disrespect you. The Bible says, "By this all men will know that you are my disciples, if you love one another" (John 13:35). Love is primarily shown through acts of kindness and genuine respect. If you show me a person who is a Christian but not kind-hearted, then I don't think you can truly say that person is a Christian. Christian love is exemplified by being respectful and kind.

In the workplace, I am not a "proselytizer." I believe that if I live my life a certain way it will attract others to Christ. I don't stick a fish symbol on my car, wear crosses around my neck, or hang religious symbols up in my office. There is nothing wrong with those displays of faith, but I would much rather have the way I live my life symbolize Christ.

It's like people who forward chain e-mails constantly. The challenge is that when they send something important, people are desensitized to it and don't pay attention. Too many people have had horrible experiences with "Christian business owners" who aren't honest or don't live up to their expectations of what it means to be a Christian in business. I don't want to be that person.

I focus on trying to be kind. It's not easy. How do you become a person who is full of respect and kindness? Two places develop and manifest respect and kindness in people's lives: their character and their judgment. Our character develops qualities through being resolute in knowing who we are in Christ. Judgment is wisdom. God tells us that if we seek him and ask for wisdom, he will give it to us, and he doesn't take it back as long as we are not double-minded.

There are going to be people who don't like me. That's okay. But it doesn't mean that I can refrain from showing those people respect and kindness. The Bible says if we are going to reign with Jesus, we have to suffer with him. I am a minority. I can't change someone who narrow-mindedly doesn't like me because of my African-American ethnicity. I know those attitudes exist, even in the church. I notice the distance people keep from me. Racism has affected me. It ticks me off. It frustrates me. But those emotions aren't productive. What is productive, and the only things I can control, are my actions and how I treat others.

COREY BELL on
GOD IN ADVERSITY (bio p. 251)

It's important that no matter what happens with your business, you still believe God is on the throne. His Word says, "I was young and now I am old, yet I have never seen the righteous forsaken or their children begging bread" (Psalm 37:25). I can hold him to his word on this. He says, "Test me in this . . . and see if I will not throw open the floodgates of heaven and pour out so much blessing that you will not have room enough for it." (Malachi 3:10). God is going to take care of us when we live in ways that are righteous and pleasing to him. I try to live that way and not wake up saying to myself, "Man, I'm going to really take advantage of someone today."

This perspective started taking shape when I was a child, the oldest of thirteen kids being raised by awesome Christian parents who loved God and his Word. I walked away from the faith for a little while, but returned and took it as my own around the time I married my wife when I was twenty-five. We married three years after my dad died and three years before my mom died. Since my mom died eight years ago, my wife and I have been raising nine of my siblings, who, at the time, ranged from ages seven to twenty. Together, we have continued walking with God, determined to accept the bumps and bruises along with the victories.

HOWARD DAHL on
SPIRITUAL GROWTH
THROUGH DIFFICULT TIMES (bio pp. 253-254)

Some of the very best times of spiritual growth and spiritual dependency came through the most difficult days of our businesses. When you go through difficulties, how you respond is a real test. Do you have a tendency to take shortcuts in either good times or bad, or do you have an ever-present sense of what God would have you do in every situation? These can be tremendous times of character shaping.

During the difficult days for Concord in the late 1980s, we would often not know at the beginning of the week how we would meet payroll on Friday. For three years God provided manna--just enough with no excess--and we never missed a payroll. This was an intense time of learning about God's power and faithfulness.

The uncertainty of business also leads us to dependency on God. There's no real presumption in business. This particular lesson is hitting home hard right now. You can have seven years of solid growth and instantly be thrown into a challenging situation where many customers can't get credit. You can never presume you know the future. It drives us to depend on God.

STEVE LYNN on
GROWTH THROUGH HARD TIMES (bio pp. 258-259)

You will find, or already know, there is something different about life's hurts when they relate to your children. I think back to the most devastating news of my life. I have a vivid recollection of my wife's call from the doctor's office to tell me that our four-year-old son had permanently lost fifty percent of his hearing through a bad case of the chicken pox. He would wear hearing aids for the rest of his life. I couldn't believe it. The absolute weight of the world was on my shoulders; however the promise I learned earlier still spoke to me. This unconditional promise that "in all things God works for the good of those who love him" (Romans 8:28) says there is a light at the end of the tunnel; there is an end to the pain; there is always hope. Call it faith if you want. The human spirit can overcome and endure unbelievable things if there is hope.

I wish it were not true, but there will be terrible, awful, very bad days in your personal and professional life. How you respond to them will determine your success in life. You will not be all that you were made to be unless there is something in your spirit that gives you hope. We must have a different view of success. We tend to put successful leaders on a pedestal and say, "They don't get scared like I do. They don't mess up like I do. They don't have morning breath like I do."

That is simply not true. To think otherwise would be to believe that Michael Jordan could do all those wonderful things with a basketball the first time he picked it up. Every great athlete who has ever lived has experienced miserable failure at some point, but what made that person great is having never given up. Likewise, the only successful leaders were at one time miserable failures who simply never gave up. Failure is just an unpleasant good—it is how we learn to search for and find success. We must think of success as the process of failing forward. I can summarize it all in one little poem:

The Real Issue

It's not how much I got or made.
Or where my name's engraved.
Nor will it ever matter,
How many clapped and raved.
There sits no jury in my gold.
No judge will see my fame.
For the tally sheet that adds me up,
Will slowly spell my name.
And after that, just one dot more;
A question will be posed.
How deeply did he share his life,
And cause this world to grow?
Did this man love?
Did this man share?
Did this man dare enough to care?

Dan Baker

BEN CHATRAW on ALLEGIANCE (bio pp. 252-253)

Business leaders are driven by vision. While passionately pursuing a vision, there is a chance we will come to a decision point where we feel we are forced to choose between maintaining our vision or following God.

Our nature as humans is to take God's direction and wrap our own personal veneer around it. Odds are it will take most of us only a few seconds to think of a pastor, politician, or business leader who utilized a Christ-centered vision for personal gain. In some cases, the vision may have been legitimate, consistent with God's Word and God's desire. However, it is often easy to manipulate and twist circumstances to use God's mission for our own personal comfort, security, or gain.

The challenge is all that more pressing when as leaders we are fighting, scraping, clawing, bleeding, and sacrificing with those around us for a moral imperative. We are fighting for God in our business, God in our families, God in our lives, but we find ourselves in a situation where following God's rules and ways seems certain to bring doom to our vision, company, job, or deal.

Most people know the great stories of David. Anointed to be king as a child, David was ordained by the Lord to lead his people. He took on lions and bears, led armies into battles, and, of course, KO'd the giant in the greatest slingshot battle known to humankind. However, I believe David's greatest victory came from inside a cave in the middle of the desert where he won a battle by not drawing a weapon.

Saul, the current King of Israel, had fallen off his rocker. David was Saul's most loyal subject, but Saul's jealously had created some pretty serious delusions. After years of sending David into impossible missions and battles and attempting to end David's life without getting his hands dirty, Saul had decided to roll up his sleeves and personally deal with the situation regardless of the cost. After David escaped to the wilderness, Saul grabbed his armies and went on a personal manhunt.

Meanwhile, David had developed quite a following of exiles and misfits. While Saul had his armies off hunting for David, David's small band defended Israelite cities from the Philistines. David moved from spot to spot, hiding in caves and the wilderness as Saul closed in.

Then one day, Saul got very close. Saul's army marched directly outside the cave where David and his men were hiding in the dark shadows of its recesses. As the army passed by, Saul had to relieve himself, and walked right into David's cave. Saul removed his clothes and his sword. Coming from desert brightness into nearly total darkness, Saul's squinting eyes could not see a thing. However, David's sight was adjusted to the cave light, and I'm sure he and his men couldn't believe what was happening. Saul was alone, without his sword, unprotected, and blinded by the darkness.

This was David's chance. God had ordained him to be king. It was his destiny. God had given David a clear vision of what could and should be, and it involved David becoming king. David had been running in the wilderness and hiding from a man God had already rejected as king, and who was determined to kill him. Hiding in caves wasn't a lot of fun, nor was it a position from which David could rule over the people of Israel and follow the path God had set out for him.

Eventually Saul's army was going to catch up with him. He couldn't run forever, and in order for him to be king, well, Saul had to "taken out of the picture."

I can only imagine the encouragement David got from his men.
> "This is your shot."
> "He's been after us for so long. He deserves to die."
> "You can end this thing now."
> "This is your once-in-a-lifetime, God-given opportunity!"

David remembered that it was the Lord who had made Saul king and concluded that attacking Saul would be the equivalent of striking at the Lord. He let Saul go, and Saul left the cave with no idea that his life had just been spared.

David could have easily looked at the circumstances, lined them up with his God-inspired vision of becoming king, and concluded that it was God's desire for him to take a shortcut. Although Saul's death at that moment certainly seemed to line up with God's ordination and David's vision for the future, doing so would have broken God's law. It was against God's rules to kill the king he had also once commanded the prophet Samuel to anoint. Had David killed Saul at that moment, he would have made a tragic mistake.

We can't allow ourselves to wrap our personal veneer around God. If we have a godly vision for our lives, our businesses, or our careers, we need to be prepared for the day when we will be presented with an opportunity to further the vision, or even capture it, by bending God's rules. Ultimately, the decision is one of allegiance—either to the vision, or to the Vision-giver.

Like David, we should put our allegiance to God in front of all things. We may have to sacrifice our plans for the future and the things we have been fighting so hard to obtain rather than bend God's rules, but that is what we must do nonetheless.

GEORGE KETTLE (as told by Mr. SPENCER BRAND) on LEADERSHIP : EXAMPLE, PERSEVERENCE, and PHILANTHROPY (bios on pp. 257 & 252, respectively)

When George Kettle was a young boy growing up in Fort Meyer, Virginia, his father, an army sergeant, was recovering at Walter Reed Hospital. In walked General George Marshall, who later commanded all of the US Armed Forces in World War II, with a poinsettia plant for George's father. Decades later, George spent almost every Christmas delivering scores of poinsettias to people.

What we experience during childhood often shapes how we relate to people as we grow older. Who affected you as a child? And who are you affecting now? In whom are you investing your time, your talent, and your treasure? Whose lives are you trying to influence?

In the New Testament, the phrase "one another" is used thirty-seven times. "Love *one another*," "forgive *one another*," "encourage *one another*," "stimulate *one another* to love and good deeds," even "bear with *one another*." Others were the focus of George's life.

Late one night while George was in high school, he and two other boys were driving home to Virginia from a swim meet in Maryland. While the trio of students stopped at an old diner for coffee and breakfast, an elderly African-American man dressed in bib overalls and toting a galvanized pail walked in. The man asked the guy behind the counter if he could buy a pot of coffee. The man behind the counter shooed the elderly man away, saying, "Get out of here; we don't serve N-----rs like you."

As the man turned and left, George saw in his downcast face something he would never forget. George sat transfixed. He did not move; he did nothing but watch. Later as George would talk about his failure to act, he would begin to tear up at the thought of that man. But out of that failure as a youth, years later God would spur George to invest in the lives of inner-city African-American children in America, young Africans in Africa, and others around the world. He gave millions of dollars, countless hours and his talent and energy providing scholarships and other programs to help children prepare for and go to college.

In his last years, George traveled to prisons all over the country and different parts of the world to talk with prisoners. They would hug him and cry with him.

One of George's favorite messages was titled "Twenty-one Things That All Successful People I Have Met in My Lifetime Have in Common." It was not "Twenty-one Secrets to My Success." What he saw in other people motivated George to excel in life. He saw that attitudes and goals mattered. He brought a positive attitude to any situation.

During George's second year as a student at the University of Maryland, his professor took him aside and said, "George, my advice is for you to drop out of school and either lay bricks or drive trucks." So George dropped out of school. He did not tell his professor that he had already developed a sales organization of fifteen to twenty people selling silver and china to young women preparing their hope chests (stocking up on things they would like to take with them into marriage). He did not tell his professor that this sales gig outfitted him with a new car. The professor could not see this young man's potential.

In contrast, a few years later, while still a salesman, George showed up at a party where he ran into a former broker. The man said, "George, if anyone could be a broker, it would be you." So George gave it a try and became successful. Later, seeing an opportunity many did not see at the time, George bought the Century 21 Real Estate franchise for the Mid-Atlantic States. Century 21 would later become the largest real estate organization in America and was sold to Cendant Corporation, providing George with a large payoff.

At one point, George and a business partner bought a large piece of ocean-front real estate, and eventually sold it for a $1.2 million profit. On closing day, George's partner did not show up to split the $1.2 million check. George called his partner's secretary and explained, "I've got a check for him. Where is he?" She answered, "I'm not going to tell you. He didn't want anyone to know." He replied, "Well, I've got $600,000 dollars that belongs to him." She said, "I know. I will let him know, and if he wants to call you, he can."

Three months passed. It turned out the partner had taken his family on an RV vacation across America. When he came back, he called George, who asked, "Where in the world have you been? I have been sitting on $600,000 of your money. Weren't you concerned?" The partner replied, "George, I didn't think that was your price."

What's your price? It's important to firmly establish the lines you will not cross, the places of integrity that won't be compromised at any price. During the years George was developing his business, he was at the same time struggling and failing in many ways as a father and husband. One day, returning from a trip to Pennsylvania, out of desperation, George pulled alongside the road and said, "Lord Jesus, if you are real, I want to know you in a way that I have heard I can know you." That day was the beginning of George's second chance at life. It was also the day he decided to give ten percent of everything he made to the Lord and to open what he called "God's Account."

As the years went by, God took this man who cried out to him at the side of a road and who as a boy had "done nothing" in that old diner so many years ago and enabled George to help thousands upon thousands of individuals before his death on April 15, 2009. In 2003, George developed his first cancerous tumor. His family thought he was going to die in the near future, but he lived another six years. Before he died, George's son, Kevin, was contemplating his dad's life and went into George's office. He found three stacks of paper piled on his desk. One stack was a pile of news periodicals, like *Newsweek* magazine and educational, informational material. Another stack contained financial briefings on George's investments.

The last stack, the tallest one, was made up of thank you notes from people like nuns in Iowa who now have a money-making fudge factory because of George, a young African-American man who graduated from college and just got married, a Caucasian girl who graduated from college, and notes from many, many other people. Few people knew George had quietly helped so many people over the years.

In the last days of your life, what will be sitting on your desktop?

what have you learned about character?

join the conversation at
www.oursoulsatwork.com/character

CHAPTER FOUR
SUCCESS

"O LORD, God of my master Abraham, if you will, please grant success to the journey on which I have come."
Genesis 24:42

Success is probably one of the most loaded words in the English language, particularly as it relates to the intersection of faith and work. In the business world, success is generally defined in terms of money and power, and little else. In the sports world, success is defined as winning. But does that translate to life? Winning at what?

Ralph Waldo Emerson reportedly said, "The line between failure and success is so fine that we scarcely know when we pass it—so fine that we often are on the line and do not know it." Success is something we strive for but cannot define well. What is success? If you took sixty seconds right now, could you formulate a sentence or two about what you think success is?

Should followers of Christ seek to be successful in the eyes of the "world"? Or is success something we should view negatively? What does success look like from a divine and biblical perspective?

Defining success is of utmost importance because it is what guides our goals, our processes, and ultimately our actions. Intuitively rejecting or accepting conventional wisdom about success is insufficient. We need to meditate on success, pray about it, discuss it with others, come to some real decisions, and then live in accordance to that definition.

MO ANDERSON on KELLER WILLIAMS REALTY: VALUES THAT FEED THE SOUL and FUEL GROWTH (bio on pp. 250-251)

People frequently ask how Keller Williams Realty has built the kind of business culture that values God and family first, and then, secondarily, business. The short answer would be that the journey began with leadership who are very grounded in their personal and business values and have never been afraid to state what those values are.

When I joined Keller Williams Realty back in 1992, I was very certain about what I believed in and what I stood for. I had some major opportunities with big-name companies, but I turned them down because their values were not compatible with mine.

The Keller Williams Realty W-I-4C-2T-S

Win-Win or no deal

Integrity do the right thing

Customers always come first

Creativity ideas before results

Commitment in all things

Communication seek first to understand

Trust starts with honesty

Teamwork together everyone achieves more

Success results through people

I thank God that I said no, because two years later, I discovered a tiny real estate company with five hundred agents in seven offices that were able to clearly articulate their values. These values, called the "WI4C2TS," serve as nine covenant agreements that guide how they do business as a company and how they treat each other.

KW Cares is a 501(c)(3) charity that raises money through Keller Williams offices across North America, in order to provide emergency financial assistance to any member of the KW family in need, as well as other charities aligned with the mission and values of Keller Williams Realty.

Nearly twenty years later, I have no doubt this little company was where I was called to be. I felt that this would be Jesus' way of running a company, and I knew in my heart that we were absolutely a match.

I believed it so strongly that I was willing to forego a salary and embraced the entrepreneurial experience that was before me. This was truly a leap of faith because, at the time, my husband and I were totally broke. The recession of the late 1980s had left us penniless.

So I turned to two of my friends, John and Paul, and asked them to loan us money. (Aren't those interesting names?) They loaned the money for one reason. They trusted my values. And so, in 1992, I opened the first region of this fledgling company that was outside of Texas.

Three years later, in 1995, having experienced a high degree of success establishing Keller Williams Realty within Oklahoma, I was asked by Gary Keller, the company's co-founder, to step up to the role of CEO and president.

I had no idea what a CEO did, so I turned him down. Gary persisted in asking me to consider this opportunity and my husband encouraged me as well. So I finally said "yes" on the condition that I could have a really low salary and a sizeable percentage of ownership in the company.

What followed was a tremendous growth journey as Keller Williams Realty grew to become the third largest real estate company in the United States, with more than 70,000 associates and close to 700 market centers throughout North America. Having replaced myself as CEO in 2005, and stepping into the role of

Vice Chairman of Keller Williams Realty and Chairman of KW Cares, it has given me great joy to observe that the WI4C2TS principles are as widely celebrated throughout our company as they have ever been.

There's no question that we have stumbled along the way, but I believe that what has strengthened our company and powered us forward is an unyielding belief in what we stand for, as well as well-defined systems and standards that provide a framework for growth.

Looking back over the past two decades, here's what I observe to be the key factors that have driven our company and our culture.

A determination to get into business with people who share our common values.

That is easier said than done, but as I once heard Ken Blanchard, author of many best-selling books, observe, "If you build a company with your values, then similar people with similar values will be attracted to it."

In addition to the WI4C2TS, our Keller Williams values are:

1) God and family first and the business second.
2) Our associates should be treated like stakeholders.
3) A stakeholder company should measure profit or loss, should open the books, and should tell the truth.
4) Profit matters. And if we're profitable, we have an obligation to share that profit with the people who helped make the profit.
5) Who we are in business with really matters.
6) No transaction is worth our reputation.

As a result of holding these values, I've had to make a lot of tough choices. When I first started my journey as president and CEO in 1995, I quickly discovered that Keller Williams Realty had gotten into business with a lot of people who did not share our values. So I began a very difficult two-year process of getting our company on the right track. There were 1,800 agents and forty offices at the time. I closed fifteen offices and got out of business with seventeen managers. It was hard, and it nearly killed my happy, fun-loving spirit.

We then set about the mission of positioning the company for growth, and that's exactly what we got. In 2002, Keller Williams Realty became the nation's seventh largest real estate company; in 2003, we were the sixth largest; the following year, we moved into the top five; in 2006 we gained Prudential's spot as number four; and in 2009 we replaced RE/MAX as the third largest real estate company in the United States. I have no doubt that we are destined to become number one.

An unapologetic statement of values and belief

Every month, I conduct a seminar for approximately two hundred prospective franchise owners, market center leaders, market center investors, and agents. I teach them how our models work, and I teach them how to launch a new market center. We call this Franchise Systems Orientation—formerly known as Launch Boot Camp.

I review our mission statement: Careers worth having—Businesses worth owning—Lives worth living. I point out that a career worth having requires profit, a business worth owning requires profit, and a life worth living will mean something different to all of us. Then I move into sharing our values, but before I begin, I let all prospective franchisees know before they consider getting into business with us that the leaders of this company are followers of Christ. And then I make a long pause. I emphasize that we are very, very proud of our diversity. If you were to ask our Muslim, Buddhist, Hindu, or Jewish agents if they feel loved and supported in our company and our culture, they would tell you "yes."

Once, two men asked for my assistance to help them negotiate a settlement for the breakup of their business. I will never forget that meeting. One of the men was Jewish. The other was Christian. I looked at both of them and said, "You worship the God of Abraham; you are a Christian. You worship the God of

Abraham; you are Jewish. I want us to take each others' hands and begin this meeting in prayer." I prayed that God would give us wisdom. I prayed that God would give them the courage to tell the truth to each other, and I prayed most of all that the friendship would be restored. It was a friendship that had begun the first day of college. God honored that prayer because those two later shared with me that they had reconciled.

I understand clearly that bringing the name of God into our business dealings is not politically correct, and I don't care. In twelve years, I have had only one person walk out highly offended that the name God or Christ had been spoken in a business seminar.

An emphasis on wealth building and stewardship

During Franchise Systems Orientation, I emphasize to all attendees that they need to be excited about building wealth, and if they are not excited about becoming wealthy, we are not a match. I point out that it is not about the money; it is about what the money can do.

I explain that we should never be afraid to pray and ask God to let us know whether we are meant to be wealthy, because it is all his and we are only the guardians for a short period of time. Once wealth comes to us, it is our obligation to ensure that we have the training and the knowledge to make sure that money is spent wisely and given away wisely.

I grew up in total poverty as the daughter of an Oklahoma sharecropper in the 1930s and 1940s. My family did not have any money, and today, there is no greater joy for me than the joy of writing out a check to someone who needs help.

Incorporate value and standards into company literature, legal documents, and training classes

Our values are repeated over and over. The leaders of our company have signature cultural stories that stand as classic demonstrations of the specific values that mean so much to our company. When a person in one of our departments comes to one of our managers and shares a moral dilemma, they are able to refer back to a story or a decision that has determined who we are as a company.

Call your people to a higher standard

Whenever I visit one of our company's regions or offices, I ask for stories that support the values that we espouse as a company.

I visited a North Carolina office several years ago and one of the agents said, "Mo, we have a great story. Joe took a listing on a property, and then proceeded to purchase it. The next day, another agent, who hadn't checked the computer to see that the property was already listed as sold, made an offer for far more money. Joe walked into his team leader's office and said, 'I have a dilemma. What do I do? If I were with my old company, I would have simply told the other agent that the property had sold, because that is all I am legally required to do, but I'm with Keller Williams now, and the WI4C2TS calls me to a higher standard.'"

Joe was exactly right. Based on the guidance from his team leader, he took the higher offer to the seller and rescinded his offer for the benefit of his client. A values-based culture changes people's behavior. Miraculously, profits and growth have followed. In fact, Keller Williams Realty has outpaced the real estate industry every step along the way. Within a matter of ten years, we grew from 2,000 agents to more than 70,000.

In 2009, during one of the most challenging real estate markets and worst economic downturns in history, we shared more than $32 million in profits with our associates. Since 1997, we've given more than $270 million back to our people in the form of profit share. Sharing market center profits with the people who have helped to make them has extended the light, love, and the opportunity of our company. I believe that our culture is at the heart of our company's phenomenal growth. It is who we are. And the growth is exciting because the sky's the limit.

There's a hunger in the hearts and minds of most of the people in this country to be affiliated with an organization that has integrity and cares about more than just profit. More people come to our company because of the culture—the regard we have for each other, our families, and our spiritual beliefs—than for any other reason.

Giving, sharing, and helping is just who we are. It's in our hearts; it's in our minds; it's at our core. Each of us is growing along with the growth of Keller Williams Realty, and together, we stand as a constellation of success.

I often find myself wondering how in the world an Oklahoma farm girl ended up as vice chairman of the third largest real estate company in the United States. I'll never fully be able to answer that question, but I do know that God has a plan for all of our lives that is greater than anything we could imagine. A lesson that I've learned over and over again in my life is that "all things work together for good, for those who are called according to his purpose" (Romans 8:28), and that there is always a spiritual lesson in adversity. My husband and I were in our 50s in the 1980s when we lost everything and had to start over again. I now realize that losing all our money was the greatest thing that ever happened to us, because it sparked the chain of events that led us to Keller Williams Realty.

BRIAN LEWIS on
SUCCESS AND FAILURE (bio p. 258)

What is perhaps least understood about success is that many successful people are burdened by it. They see what they have accomplished, but it feels small compared to what they hoped might have been possible. The story is the same, whether it is the councilman who becomes a state senator but is never elected to Congress; the president elected with great fanfare but leaves office with the ambitions of his first years largely unfulfilled; the best-selling author who achieves financial acclaim, but her work is never taken seriously for its literary merit; or the esteemed scientist, who never holds the Nobel Prize.

Once I worked with a CEO who had made a long journey from a modest beginning. He was now leading a nearly $200 million a year global company. Yet, in his quiet moments, he would tell me, "My friends from business school now lead billion-dollar firms. They run publicly-traded companies." Success has its satisfactions, but also its own set of burdens.

This is why success should always be held lightly, for it is squirrelly. Winning has a way of producing a temporary euphoria that recedes quickly and routinely, like the tide. This is why *defining* success—understanding what we personally mean by this word—is one of the most important tasks of our lives. It can be a waste to run hard for a goal that you discover was never what you hoped it would be. Ideally, we should clearly define "success" for ourselves at the outset of our careers, but this rarely occurs. Typically, we define success as we live life on the run.

Developing a thoughtful understanding of failure is just as important as defining success. Failure is often calibrated to the scale of our ambitions. Fear of failure can cause ambitions to be miniaturized. If someone's ambitions are audacious, there will be a certain inevitability of failure.

One of the great pities is when superior talent is joined with inferior ambitions. This is why each of us should experience some measure of failure. If we never fail, perhaps it is because our ambitions have been miniaturized. Perhaps unbroken success should rouse our suspicions.

Leaders of philanthropic organizations in particular should respect the way in which success and failure is calibrated to outsized or miniaturized ambitions. For many years, I have worked with HOPE International (HI) on its board of trustees. HI is a Christian organization seeking to "invest in the dreams of the poor" through micro-enterprise loans. In its mission statement, HI says that it intends to "work in the hard places of the world"—to pick the places where the obstacles are greatest, the governments most unstable, and where people have experienced the most chronic disappointment. What you can expect from an organization that works in the easy places is perhaps different from what you can expect from an organization that chooses life in the hard places. Failure, as much as success, should be measured in conjunction with levels of ambition.

Indeed, a thoughtful approach to failure is an intrinsic part of "good process." For many years I have worked with Scandinavian companies, and during weekends in Stockholm often visited the old town section called *Gamla stan*. On the cobblestone streets of this historic district is a handsome building housing the Nobel Museum, which celebrates the winners of the Nobel Prize.

The Nobel Museum chronicles how great leaps forward in science typically occur. Progress is almost always an intermittent process—one step forward is followed by two steps backward, and then another step forward. The Nobel landscape is the story of how scientists and artists who take journeys worth taking use failure.

Great discoverers *study* failure to understand why dead ends are dead ends, why some doors close and other doors open. Great discoverers expect failure and never fear it. Failure is not denied or disguised; rather, failure is analyzed and followed to see where it might lead, to learn what secrets it has to reveal.

As Christians, we know failure is often not what it seems. What seemed to be the day of greatest failure—the crucifixion of Jesus—was not the end of the story. The great discovery—the resurrection of Jesus—lay just around the corner. This is in part why Christians should be among those most comfortable with acknowledging reality. There should be less need for pretending in us. Yet sometimes, even with Christian leaders, fear of failure leads to a bending of reality, and the distortions of a bad process.

Many years ago, a publicly-traded company hired me to evaluate their prospective new marketing campaign. The CEO had built a large enterprise and was a person of faith, yet he had created a culture that suffered from candor-deficit disorder. After I entered the boardroom and offered my thoughts to the CEO and his team, I watched as the team waited, waited—and then waited some more—for the CEO to speak, so they could calibrate their views to his. This was a company culture that would eventually stumble, because when candor is an at-risk behavior, the mistakes of groupthink often follow. A culture that disguises failure is always at greater risk than a culture that looks for its lessons. One of our goals should be an inner freedom that allows us to be the most-candid, most honest people in the room in our respective organizations.

In contrast, some company cultures use failure as a competitive strength. One of the leaders of a Swedish client has often said failure is his company's great moment of opportunity. It is when a product fails, my colleague says, that a customer learns the truth about the culture of their suppliers. In the case of my Swedish client, failure is the moment of truth when customers see whether marketing language about "never walking away from a problem" is true in real life. This company's most abiding customer relationships have always resulted from failures.

Many of the great turning-point decisions in our lives will be shaped by how we understand these ideas of success and failure. As Christians, we are told we must build our lives on rock, not sand, yet recognizing which is which in "real time" is not always easy. What is the sand, and what is the rock? Those of us in mid-career or late-career may have the luxury of re-balancing our lives to bring them into better alignment, but young people entering demanding careers—law, medicine, business—tend to inevitably find themselves in the eye of the storm. Significant achievement in these careers can require a focus of time and attention that is inherently unbalancing.

What then can we hope for? We can expect to at times make poor decisions, but we can learn to not get stuck. We can expect that our definitions of success will be tested, and perhaps changed. We can expect to fail, but we can learn to fail well, because our ambitions are properly proportioned. We can strive for the inner freedom that will allow us to be some of the most honest, most candid people in the room.

HARRI SUNDVIK on
A DEFINITION OF SUCCESS (bio p. 267)

The best definition I've found for success is a statement John Maxwell makes in his book *The 360 Degree Leader*. He says, "Success is having those closest to me love and respect me the most." It's a fascinating and challenging definition.

Sadly, particularly in the executive world, the temptation is to allow what corporate people say, or being featured in a prominent magazine, or receiving a distinguished award to become your measure of success. So remember, *success is when the people who know me the best love and respect me the most.*

HENRY KAESTNER on
DOING THE RIGHT THING (bio pp. 256-257)

As David Morken and I were starting Bandwidth.com, we were more than eager for business clients to buy Internet access from us. In January 2001, we shifted our model from lead referral—where we sent interested businesses directly to carriers—to one of agency—where we transacted the business directly with customers—and we weren't sure it would work. To make matters worse, 2001 was quite possibly the worst time in recent history to raise money from outside investors. The Internet bubble had just burst and telecommunications companies had fallen out of favor. Imagine a new start up that was a telecom dotcom! It took us three and a half months to get our first customer and times were lean. We were eager for leads. We were eager for customers, and we were desperate to make payroll. One type of buyer came to us over and over again, ready, willing, and able to buy large quantities of Internet access from us with the cash to make it happen. One of the largest consumers of bandwidth was—and still is—the adult entertainment industry.

This sector and its ready cash loomed above us like a Jezebel with the promise of relief from our short-term cash woes. We made a firm decision not to call back any leads of suspicious origin and made our policy clear to our sales representatives. Several times after celebrating wins with our team, we unilaterally cancelled the deal because we found the buyer we thought was legitimate was a front for a pornography business. Those losses were very hard; however, David and I were resolute in our decision that, no matter how much we needed cash, we would never, ever do anything to assist an industry responsible for tearing apart so many lives and families.

Through God's grace and providence, Bandwidth.com was able to get through that perilous time and become the fastest growing telecom company over the last five years, and the fourth fastest growing privately held company of any kind. David and I are not perfect stewards of the gifts God has given us and have made many mistakes along the way; we are indeed fallen men in a fallen world. But we have committed our lives and our business to God and try to be as faithful as we can possibly be. We believe our reliance on Him, especially through the challenging times in the early days of the company is the reason for our success. We pray he will continue to give us the strength to be good and faithful servants and to use our success for his glory.

WENDY MURPHY on
COMPETITION (bio p. 262)

If I can get one message across, it's go out into the marketplace and be the best you can be. Go the distance, push, and be competitive. The Christian life is competitive, and I'm fiercely competitive. Go out there and be the best. Be salt and light in the marketplace because it keeps us all edgy, and I believe that Christians need to be edgy; we need to be smart and about excellence in everything.

WENDY MURPHY on
COMPETING AS A WOMAN (bio p. 262)

As a woman at this level, you have to prove yourself twice as much as a man. Your ideas must be extremely logical, well-grounded, and you can't use one bit of feminine wiles to project them or you will be labeled manipulative. On every business trip, a woman has to watch herself. I interview male candidates all the time, and I have to make sure there are no mixed messages, that I set clear boundaries. Our words, speech, and conduct must line up. We're in a changing world, and it's a free for all. Morals aren't what they were twenty years ago. It's constantly an issue. I practice some clear disciplines when I travel. I never eat dinner out; I go up to my room and order room service. If I am interviewing a male candidate, it will be between 6:00 and 8:00 pm—and that's the end of it. Those are pretty rigorous disciplines, but if you don't adhere to them, the message you send will be taken the wrong way. If you are careful, nothing disparaging can be said of you.

As a woman, you won't be having a beer with the boss. You will have to have all of your ducks in a row, every penny squared away. It is what it is, and it doesn't depend on the boss or the organization. I'm on our management team, but I still make sure every detail is accurate. You may come in with your business plan in perfect order, and because there are two guys who had a beer together last night, it's already done. What do you do? It's hard, but the extra effort we must put in hones us, it makes us better, so ultimately when we're standing before a client or with a group of CEOs, we know our stuff cold.

I do believe that women are continually breaking through barriers. I have a great mentor in the candidate search business. She's in her late fifties. When I complain, she says, "Wendy, if you only knew what we went through. . . ." You've got to keep it together, and be better at what you do than the next guy. You are in a team environment. It isn't the boys against the girls, although sometimes it feels that way.

If you look at people through the Lord's eyes, it makes it a little bit easier. When you feel better than someone or they seem to be an enemy, remember that Jesus loves that person as much as he loves you. It puts things into perspective.

TYLER SELF on
TWO ESSENTIAL QUALITIES FOR SUCCESS (bio p. 266)

If you were given the opportunity to be endowed with two qualities critical to business success, which would you choose? Would you prefer the super-intelligence of a Nobel scholar combined with a handsome face? Perhaps the credibility of a world leader combined with uncanny sales and marketing acumen? What must one have to establish a successful company that thrives over the long term?

In 1946, at a small restaurant outside of Atlanta, Truett Cathy and his brother, Ben, sat exhausted one Saturday evening after covering six twenty-four-hour shifts between the two of them. The founder of Chick-fil-A® decided to close the restaurant the next day, and over the sixty-three years since, every Chick-fil-A® restaurant has closed its doors on Sunday.

Some doubt that any restaurant could survive without the most important sales day of the week, and some have marveled that Chick-fil-A® could thrive in spite of the lost day, yet Truett Cathy asserts that the business has grown because of that decision. He reminds others of the fourth commandment: to work six days and reserve the seventh for rest. His decision may be the one thing that has set the company apart. God honored Mr. Cathy for his obedience in this area and many other areas of his life.

I was privileged to spend an afternoon with Mr. Cathy a few years ago, and it became clear to me that he possessed two essential ingredients for success. You will find these two qualities in any successful investor.

The first is wisdom: the wisdom to know what to do and what to avoid. The second is confidence: the confidence to take action on wisdom. Mr. Cathy had the wisdom to close his restaurants on Sunday, but more importantly, he had the confidence to step out in faith and lock the doors.

The most substantial investor in my business is a highly revered money manager in Texas. He spoke to me a few years ago of one of his investments in a small private company in California. The company is now very large and very well known, and his original risk was extremely profitable. What did it take to multiply the investment many times over? It took the wisdom to know that the opportunity was a good investment and the confidence to take hard-earned money and entrust it to the company's founders, nothing more. He has applied this simple formula over and over with extraordinary success.

The amazing revelation about wisdom and confidence is, as children of God, we have unlimited access to both through our relationship with Christ. In James 1:5, the Lord promises to give his perfect wisdom to whoever asks of it by faith. David said in Psalm 27 that he found his confidence in the Lord.

As a young entrepreneur, I recognize that my wisdom is relatively low on the scale; thus, I must pray daily in faith for wisdom. Others may find that confidence wanes as the years pass, and they must pray daily for confidence. Solomon chose wisdom and became famous among the kings and queens of his day, and he has remained known for his wisdom ever since. If we ask the Father through faith, he will freely and generously pour out both wisdom and confidence.

STEVE LYNN on
A SUCCESSFUL JOURNEY (bio pp. 258-259)

I grew up on the proverbial other side of the tracks in a little southwestern Georgia cotton-mill town. For as far back as I can remember I wanted to get to the other side, to the kind of housing I saw there, to air conditioning, good food, and cleanliness. I have also always wanted to be the CEO of a company. Not because I understood exactly what that meant; rather, because the owners and leaders of companies in my hometown took an interest in me, and I wanted to be like them.

I have always been very driven. I went to college on an athletic scholarship, graduated with an engineering degree, did my MBA at the University of Louisville, and began my career. At twenty-nine, I became president of a company and married my wife, Milah. I had achieved a major life goal and had some of what the great American dream is all about: a nice California house, pool, wife, sheepdog, and Mercedes. But I was respectfully ignoring my new trophy wife—she wasn't a full partner in my life. Being president of the company was all that mattered.

Then one day, life, in the form of Milah, grabbed me by the shoulders, shook me, and caused me to slow down long enough to focus on my priorities. Standing in the foyer of that California house, she asked me, "What are the most important things in your life?" I responded, "Power, recognition, and money." A look of pain crossed her face. I'm a salesman by nature and fast on my feet, so I added, "Darling, it goes without saying that you're number one." But she knew the truth.

We lived an hour and a half away from my work. There is something therapeutic about long drive times; they give you time to reflect. So I started thinking about life, my priorities, and our wedding vows on my next trip to the office. I realized our vows meant absolutely nothing to me. I just repeated what the pastor said without thinking about them. I hadn't made a genuine commitment.

A few months later, driving to work, I made an unconditional commitment that I was going to spend the rest of my life with Milah—a choice that simplified and changed everything. For example, externally, I am a low-key, laid-back, southern gentleman, but internally, I am a hard-driving competitor. When we had disagreements, I won them all; that was my nature. I endured until she gave up. But if I wanted to spend the rest of my life with this lady, that wouldn't work. There had to be a win-win partnership.

Physical beauty was important to me, and she was and is beautiful. But God, time, and gravity take care of this physical beauty for us all. How would I happily grow old with her? I refocused my view on what attracts me to her, so, like a great bottle of wine, she only got better with age. This unconditional commitment was a major step for a self-centered, ambitious, ex-athlete like myself. It was the first time in my life I made a commitment to anything or anyone that didn't focus on "What's in it for me?"

Growing up I never went to church. When Milah and I began irregularly attending a large Presbyterian church near our home, I didn't know the rules. I didn't know when to stand up or sit down; whether to sing all four verses or just the first and third. It was boring. But we started going to a large class of young married couples like us. A tall basketball-type guy from the class began to visit me. He was on staff with Campus Crusade. I could play basketball with him, elbow him, try to beat him, and discovered Christians weren't pushovers. This was a new revelation for me.

I decided to prove to him and me that God didn't exist. We met for a whole year about this; he was very loving and patient. I would ask questions like, "How could a God of love let my friend's mother suffer with cancer for three years before she died?" As the year wore on, I didn't get all of my questions answered, but somehow they got less important. At the same time, through my father-in-law, a Christian businessman, I was discovering you could be successful and still love the Lord—also a new revelation for me.

Once again, driving to work, I had a change of heart and said a simple, naïve, inadequate prayer and turned my life over to Jesus. There were no voices. I didn't feel any different. But as the days, weeks, and months went by, my life changed from the inside out. My marriage was healed and blessed, work became less important, and I felt like I did a better job at it.

However, when Jesus captures our hearts, the promise isn't that it will all be easy. The promise is that we belong to him, and he'll be there whatever comes. Two months later, my company's parent sold and a representative of the new owners called me into his office. An hour and a half later, I left his office remembering only two words, "You're fired." At twenty-nine, I had achieved my life's major goal, and at thirty-two, it felt like it was ripped away from me.

While I was out of work for several months, I experienced the bruised ego, frustration, self-doubt, confusion, and anger that anyone goes through when they lose something precious. Two weeks after being fired, my brother-in-law called to tell me that my father had shot and killed himself. One of the men who had been instrumental in leading me to this newfound faith, called to share his condolences. He shared Romans 8:28 (NKJV), "We know that all things work together for good to those who love God." It did not make me feel any better. But, as the days went by, and I combined my new faith with this unconditional promise, I came to believe that no matter what I went through, there was hope. For over thirty years now, this verse has helped me through the "bumps in the road" that life deals us all.

I became reemployed as COO for a Los Angeles-based restaurant chain. During this time, Milah and I went to Campus Crusade for Christ headquarters for a one-week training session for business executives and their spouses. One of Sonic's largest franchisees and his wife were attending and we became friends. Upon returning home, he recommended me to Sonic's founder, Troy Smith. When he retired, I was brought in to take his place.

A different view of success

The company was in a state of decline. Sales had dipped below $200 million. Sonic was a publicly-traded company with a market value of $5 million. The company had closed over four hundred stores in the four years before I arrived, as well as experiencing four straight years of same store sales decline. None of our 930 stores in eighteen states advertised or purchased together. It was an old, weary, fifties-style carhop business with lots of deferred maintenance. Average annual store sales were only $210,000. We owned and operated 110 stores that were losing $1.5 million a year.

We had an old, out-dated license agreement with our franchisees. The agreement had no required advertising fund and collected the royalty as a fixed mark-up on our paper goods. It had no inflation factor built in and had started out as a reasonable royalty twenty-nine years earlier but by this time had declined to about .5 percent of sales. A typical industry royalty is three to six percent of sales. The chain was surviving essentially by the entrepreneurial gumption of our franchisees. Legally, we were a public company; functionally, we were a private company owned by the twelve men who sat on my Board of Directors. They were multi-unit franchisees who owned seventy-two percent of Sonic. Less than ten percent of our stores had cash registers, so we were not getting meaningful purchasing and marketing data. And our operators did not know we were going out of business.

Being thirty-six and too ignorant to know it couldn't be fixed, I went to Sonic with a lot of enthusiasm. Strategically, the three most important issues were: First, to get the chain united in advertising and purchasing and operating like a chain. If we could not accomplish this nothing else mattered. Second, to put a new royalty licensing agreement in place—otherwise, as we fixed the chain, the franchisor would not reap its share of the rewards. Third, the most urgent thing was to stop the annual hemorrhage of a million and a half dollars in company-owned stores.

We focused on the markets where we had a critical mass of stores, such as Joplin/Pittsburgh, Missouri and Jackson, Mississippi. The franchisees in each market would come together for a day. I would graphically prove to them that we were going out of business. Once I could see reality dawn in their eyes, I would say, "The good news is, we are going out of business slowly, and, if you will take a step of faith with me, we can fix this together." The objective was to establish twenty-one advertising/purchasing co-ops in about one-third of our system and show the rest of our operators the power of uniting in order to create a critical mass that would drive same-store sales growth and reduce food cost. Further they were required to sign up at least seventy-five percent of the stores in that co-op's marketplace.

We knew critical mass in each co-op was a necessity. I asked the franchisees to sign a simple six-page legal document committing to each other to form a purchasing and advertising co-op for one year. They would purchase from one distributor of the co-op's choice and commit to spend one percent of sales on advertising. After a year of hard work, we did not have twenty-one co-ops formed, but we had seventeen and put our complete focus on making those perform.

Increasing the royalty was a political challenge because the majority of our stock was owned by franchisees. The way we sold this was to convert to an industry standard percent of sales royalty but make it a graduated scale. So we started at .5 percent (about what they were paying) and went up to four percent as sales went up.

The third piece, the most urgent piece, was fixing the bleeding in company-owned stores. We required the managers of the 110 company-owned locations to buy twenty-five percent of their unit, essentially converting them to partners and the CEO of their store. Turnover rate went from 110 percent a year to eight percent.

Owner-managers became the star of the show at annual conventions. The first "Manager of the Year" was a little five-foot six-inch guy in Southern Kentucky. His store showed two years of positive sales. On a $28,000 annual salary, he made $240,000. What did that say to every other manager in the audience? "If he can do it, I can do it!" It was a magical thing. I asked how he did it. "I reached a point of understanding that this was my business and not yours," he replied. "I reached a point of more fear about failure than fear of people. I got out of my store and everywhere I went I was the Sonic brand." Local store marketing exploded in a positive way.

By the time I left twelve years later, ninety-eight percent of the chains purchased together and ninety-four percent of the chains advertised together. Average store sales moved from $210,000 to breaking all industry records for consecutive years of same-store sales growth, and currently average about $1.1 million per store. The year before I left, *Success* magazine chose this old, weary, worn out, fifties-style restaurant chain as the number one franchise opportunity in the world. And in recent years, Sonic has reached a market value of about $2.3 billion. It was a wonderful run. Again, I say turnarounds are a "we" thing, not a "me" thing.

Because of the way God blessed us at Sonic, I was invited to take on another turnaround challenge: Shoney's and Capt. D's, headquartered in Nashville, Tennessee. Over my three years at Shoney's, we put together a new management team and strategic plan. We were chipping away at it. Shoney's same-store sales had dropped significantly in the four years before my arrival. By my final eighteen months, we moved that to negative one percent with occasional positive months. We moved health inspection scores from a miserable sixty-seven to a healthy eighty-nine, and our stock price from about $7 to $13.

Could we have fixed it? I don't know. However, the co-founders owned eighteen percent of the company and were impatient about the turnaround. They began an effort to regain control of the company through a proxy battle. A few months into the battle, we reached a negotiated settlement. After this, I decided to depart the company. In the world's eyes Sonic was enormously successful and Shoney's was not. But in my heart, I had some of the most fun and did some of the best work of my career at Shoney's.

KATHERINE FOO on
IDENTITY IN CHRIST (bio pp. 254-255)

"Be careful in what, or who, you let define you." My last supervisor gave me this advice after a frustrating incident with a client. It is among the most memorable pieces of advice I have ever received.

As we deal with life, we pump ourselves up by telling ourselves things like, "I helped my division increase profits by 260 percent!" or "I demonstrated my ingenuity by devising a way to expand our market." Suddenly, we are the bomb! There are many accomplishments that you may justifiably feel proud about.

However, as Christians, we should not be defined by our achievements, no matter how amazing they sound, or by the fact that we go to a top-tier business school. It may also be tempting to let our identity be affected by our dream company or by our interviewers as we seek to further our careers; rather, we should remember that our identity is based on Christ. He is our worth, joy, and where our hope should come from.

When we start placing too much attention on certain things or people, or when we are upset when something is taken away or when an interview goes unexpectedly wrong, perhaps it is a sign that we need to focus our eyes on Christ once more and to reclaim our identity. There is good reason to have confidence and feel awesome, but may we allow God *alone* to define us.

how do you define success?

join the conversation at
www.oursoulsatwork.com/success

CHAPTER FIVE
MONEY

$

"No one can serve two masters. Either he will hate the one and love the other, or he will be devoted to the one and despise the other. You cannot serve both God and Money."
Matthew 6:24

These words of Christ are as challenging as they are confusing. I'm always suspicious when I hear someone say they don't care about money. "How do you live without it?" I want to ask. Nevertheless, Christ's words hang in the air, needing to be dealt with. If there is one criticism of business, it's that it's all about the money. Jesus is saying we need to be all about God.

Money is something we all need, and most of us have to work for it. If entrepreneurs and executives did not go to work everyday creating wealth, human suffering would be the inevitable result. Our basic life necessities, such as food, shelter, and water, all require money. As we move beyond these basic necessities to other valuable activities, like education, transportation, hobbies, family trips, more money is needed. How do we reconcile this reality with what Jesus says?

Deep down most of us want more money than we need. Therein lies the tension—we need money, yet we want even more. When it comes to money, motivation and focus are significant issues. If we work solely for money, then we have not understood the divine and spiritual purposes for work. If all we seek is money, then we are never satisfied. They say John Rockefeller, the world's first billionaire, was asked how much money it takes to make one happy. "A little bit more," he supposedly replied.

Money is like air. It is necessary for survival but should not define our purpose. If we are living to breathe, are we really even living? If we are living for money, are we spiritually alive?

Due to its centrality to our lives, money is a topic on which we should begin to formulate some serious thoughts. Conclusions regarding money are hard to come by, but the goal of this chapter is to get the conversation moving in the right direction.

TEAL CARLOCK and MAX ANDERSON on
A HIPPOCRATIC OATH FOR BUSINESS - VALUE VERSUS PROFITS
(bios on pp. 252 & 250, respectively)

To contemporary readers, Genesis 15 is surely one of the strangest portraits of God's relationship with people. God and Abraham are having a conversation. At one point, God tells Abraham, "I will bless you." Abraham, perhaps skeptical, replies, "How do I know?" God responds, "Go and kill some animals. Cut the animals into pieces and arrange the pieces in two rows with an aisle so you can walk through them."

Come again?

God's reply is utterly confusing to contemporary readers. However Abraham was not confused. He may have been skeptical about God's promise, but he showed no skepticism toward God's strange command regarding the animals. Why?

In those days, when a great lord wanted to make a covenant with a peasant or servant, he had the servant kill some animals and cut them in half. When the servant took the oath of loyalty to the lord, the servant walked between the pieces to dramatize the potential curse of the covenant. The servant effectively said, "I swear loyalty to you, oh lord, and if I do not keep my promise, may I be cut into pieces like this."

Though our culture has stopped using the dramatic imagery of such oaths, we have not given up on oath taking. When you testify in court, you take an oath to tell the truth, the whole truth, and nothing but the truth. When you get married, you take an oath to love your spouse as long as you both shall live, regardless of the circumstances. When a new president takes office, he swears an oath to defend the Constitution. As a society, we continue to ask people to make public pronouncements of their promises whenever they take on a duty of great consequence.

Implicitly, we believe in the power of vows to bind people to their commitments. Oaths matter.

Doctors take the Hippocratic Oath to "do no harm." Attorneys make oaths to uphold justice and defend their clients. Engineers take oaths to make the best use of the earth's resources. Indeed, one of the hallmarks of a profession is a widely adopted set of principles that govern the practice of the profession.

Around the turn of the twentieth century, the business school movement was launched to create graduate education for managers in the hopes of turning management into a proper profession. That vision has not yet been fulfilled, and in the wake of the global financial meltdown, it is time to reconsider it.

A hippocratic oath for managers

When you walk into a doctor's office, it is reassuring to see a medical degree hanging on the wall. *"Ahh. This person knows what he is doing. I can trust this person."* Although there are unfortunate exceptions, your baseline assumption is that the doctor's primary goal is to restore you to health; however, you don't get that same reassurance when you walk into a businessperson's office and see an MBA degree on the wall. What if you did? That is the fundamental question we are asking with the MBA Oath (see Appendix), an initiative we launched with a team of thirty classmates at Harvard Business School in the spring of 2008.

As we prepared to graduate, it seemed that every article about MBAs was snarky and skeptical. The press treated the financial meltdown as a crime against humanity, and MBAs were the prime suspects. After investing two years and tens of thousands of dollars earning our degrees, we were lumped together as a bunch of self-absorbed schemers and scoundrels. Although we feel the criticism went too far, it was quite accurate in diagnosing a major problem: we have lost a sense of duty in business that calls us to a higher standard of behavior and a higher goal than our own enrichment.

Fraud or illegal behavior did not trigger the financial crisis. Unfortunately, it was caused by firms doing business in a way that was legal, but often unwise and unethical. When business says it is the job of government to regulate behavior, it abdicates responsibility and leaves open the possibility that government will fail again. The MBA Oath is an opportunity for managers to make a commitment to a set of professional standards that acknowledge the responsibility managers have to steward the enormous influence business has in society.

Why is the oath important?

The public's distrust of business has risen to record levels. If business does not self-regulate, someone else will do it for us. We need business leaders with the wisdom to see that their motto should not be "maximize shareholder value," but "maximize the creation of responsible value."

It has been said that in the past few decades something has happened to America's attitude toward money similar to what happened in the 1960s to America's attitude toward sex. It went from being a privilege—which should be treated properly lest it corrupt you—to a commodity of infinite potential value—you should get as much as you can anyway you can.

Perhaps the strongest argument for the MBA Oath, from a Christian point of view, is that it reorients our concept of the purpose of work. You can think of the Christian understanding of work like gardening. After all, gardening is the work we were called to in Eden. As Tim Keller suggests, when you are a gardener, you don't pave over everything.

On the other hand, gardeners are not park rangers, telling people not to touch anything. A gardener takes the raw material of the earth and uses it—rearranges it to grow food and provide for human flourishing. In business we should take the raw material of human effort, ingenuity, and the earth's resources and use them to make the world better than it was before.

Just as believers advocate for political reforms that correspond with their beliefs, believers in business ought to be leaders of reforms that correspond with God's calling to business people.

As Christians in business, we have an obligation to God to carry out his commands in our daily lives. This does not seem as easy as it would be if you were a missionary, preacher, or had some other more religiously-based occupation. Our choice to lead careers in business carries both responsibility and potential. Whether you are humble to co-workers, loving to subordinates, or simply exhibiting the love of Christ in your daily walk, you are becoming the leader God intended you to be.

The business community in the United States and around the world is a fertile ground to sow the seeds of God into any mission field in an underdeveloped country. The people we interact with on a daily basis can be as lost, hungry for love, and eager to find something that will provide them lasting satisfaction as anyone else. As Christian business leaders, it is our responsibility to show Christ's love for others through letting his love run through us.

Whether Christian or not, the signers, pledgers, and fans of the MBA Oath are publicly taking a stand to make business decisions with a broader mindset rather than thinking solely of their shareholders, themselves, or their pocketbooks. We believe this ties closely with the teachings of the book of James about faith and works; those who are truly Christian will act on what they truly believe. As the number of people taking a stand and signing the oath grows, we are reminded of how thirsty people are to band together behind something seemingly more "moral," something broader than their own narrow ambitions.

A pastor said, "The purpose of work is not to feel good about yourself, get an identity, or make money: it is to create the flourishing of human community." Profit is a good thing, but it is not the only thing. Producing valuable goods and services that satisfy your customers is something that matters. Treating the people you work with like human beings who bear the image of God also matters.

The purpose of work is to see people flourish. It is an opportunity for people to use their God-given talents to create something of value for others that none of them could have created alone. In doing so, they glorify God and become participants in completing the work of creation. As Paul writes in Colossians 3:23-24, "Whatever you do, work at it with all your heart, as working for the Lord, not for men, since you know that you will receive an inheritance from the Lord as a reward. It is the Lord Christ you are serving."

We think the major commitments of the MBA Oath are all aligned with this understanding of the purpose of work. We propose that managers should:

- **Consider the purpose of business to create value.** Making a profit is wonderful, but it is the means, not the ends.
- **Conduct business ethically and with integrity.** This is the baseline of any Christian life.
- **Safeguard the interests of people affected by our decisions.** We are called to love our neighbors as ourselves and to care for "the least of these" (Matthew 25:40).
- **Avoid advancing self at the expense of the greater good.** The rich young ruler failed to follow Christ because he could not let go of the stranglehold his wealth had on him. (See Luke 18:18-23.)
- **Obey the letter and the spirit of the law.** We should render unto Caesar what is Caesar's, and where we see injustice and human law that does not align with God's law, we should work to repair it.
- **Develop ourselves and those younger than us.** We ought to follow the pattern of the disciples in investing in learning and in teaching others.
- **Seek sustainable economic, social, and environmental prosperity worldwide.** The call of the Garden of Eden isn't a call to radical environmental activism, but it is a call to steward God's resources. This pledge admits that we have a duty to "our neighbors," be they Americans, Samaritans, or a poor child laboring in India.

- **Hold each other accountable.** These values cannot be lived in isolation but must be lived in community.

We believe that Christians ought to be living these values in their work, whether or not they take the Oath. We do not think you have to be a Christian to live by these values. Nor do we think that you need to take the Oath to live by these values. However we do think the Oath helps nudge you in the right direction.

Matthew 5:37 teaches us to "let your 'yes' be 'yes,' and your 'no,' 'no.'" We don't think this is a prohibition on making promises so much as it is a warning not to double deal, and then appeal to heaven for a bail out. The MBA Oath is a statement of aspiration to remind each person of the standards by which they will operate in their professional lives. It is secondarily a promise to others. The key is to not make the promise without taking the necessary action to back it up.

Back to Abraham

The amazing thing about the story of the covenant between Abraham and God in Genesis 15 is that Abraham did not walk between the pieces of the animals, symbolizing his oath. Instead, God walked between them on his behalf! In a sermon, Rev. Tim Keller describes it this way:

> God appeared as a smoking, fiery pillar just like at Mount Sinai later on. And he passed through the pieces, as he promised to bless Abraham! Now Abraham was startled and almost every commentator who's ever tried to come to grips with Genesis 15 is startled, because what that means is that God is not just saying, "I will bless you," but he's promising to die if he doesn't bless him. He's promising to be torn to pieces if he doesn't bless Abraham. Well, that's amazing, but that's not all.
>
> "Oh Abraham, Abraham," God is saying, and to all of us, "Oh world, I will bless you no matter what. Even if it means that my immortality must become mortal. Even if my glory must drown in

darkness. Even if I have to literally be torn to pieces." And he was, because centuries later, darkness came down on Mount Calvary, thick darkness, and in the midst of the darkness there was God in the person of Jesus Christ, and he was literally being torn to pieces. Nails, spears, thorns . . . why? He was taking the covenant curse.

And it's Paul who says, "Christ redeemed us from the curse of the Law by becoming a curse for us. . . . He redeemed us in order that the blessing given to Abraham might come to us all through Jesus Christ" (Galatians 13:3,4, paraphrase). Paul says in Romans 4 this is how God can be both just and justifier of those who believe. This is the ultimate blend of law and love.

When you see the love of God made flesh like that, you can have the courage to work not out of fear, greed, or status seeking, but out of gratitude and love. When we understand the love of Christ, we realize God made good on his pledge to us. Now, we can have the radical kind of thankfulness that might enable us to make good on our pledges to him. We owe a debt we can never repay, but out of thanksgiving and joy we can work in a way that delights God, values his people and his creation, and seeks to use the gifts he has given us not for our own self-puffery and aggrandizement, but for his glory.

DAVID MILLER on
MONEY (bio pp. 260-261)

There is a danger in Christian thinking that, if you are faithful and righteous, and follow God's commands and teachings, he will bless you. God does want to bless us beyond our wildest imagination, but if that is the only voice we are reading from the Bible, my mentor, John Stott, would say, we are doing "selective dipping." We are taking only verses we want to see and we miss the verses about the sweat of our brow, the rain falling on the just and the unjust, servant leadership, and sacrificial giving for the other. The prosperity gospel is a very thin theology and dangerous spiritual veneer. Watch out for that; it is very tempting, particularly if you've experienced times of need. There is nothing wrong with wanting to take care of your family without worrying about where your next meal is coming from, but you can very easily start worshiping money thinking that it is the only thing God cares about.

STEVE REINEMUND on
CEO COMPENSATION (bio p. 264)

As the former CEO of PepsiCo, I am probably not objective enough to properly evaluate the debate over whether CEOs and executives are paid too much. I do believe, however, over the next few years, this debate is going to take an interesting course, and I hope it doesn't over-correct.

Yes, there have been abuses, but, the capitalistic system, when run by ethical people, will find a proper balance. If the public arena gets too tarnished on the issue of executive pay, I think we will see behaviors that are not in the best interest of the US economy. Already, a lot of people are moving towards private equity because they are tired of dealing with the nuisances that are out there.

Fundamentally more important is what I believe to be the biggest single world issue—the growing divide between the "haves" and "have-nots." That is a much more difficult issue, and one we all need to be part of trying to change.

KEN ELDRED on
THE MYTH THAT POVERTY IS NOBLE (bio p. 254)

It is a commonly held myth that Christians ought to embrace poverty as if poverty is somehow noble. If a person makes any money, it becomes a guilt trip. You don't really want to talk about your business success. The impact of this myth is probably best illustrated in a note a young man wrote me:

> *I wish I had read your book four years ago. I became a Christian during my first year at the MIT business school program. I believed I had to leave business and go to the mission field. Making money was just not appropriate. I just came back a year ago after three years in the Philippines, and I returned a broken man. This wasn't what I was supposed to do. Now I am working as a consultant for a major company just trying to get my feet back on the ground.*

When we buy into conventional wisdom, whether it is supported by the church or not, and we don't check it against Scripture, we end up going to places where we should not.

When the Soviet Union developed in the 1900s, the Christian community bought into the nobility of poverty, that everyone should have the same thing. People look at the world with rose-colored glasses—a tint that isn't natural. We embraced the idea that business is a zero-sum game. What is that? Poker is the perfect example of a zero-sum game. Everybody starts with the same number of chips. However, when the game is over somebody's got more and others have less. That is not what God created in business. Deuteronomy 8:18 says, "Remember the LORD your God, for it is he who gives you the ability to produce wealth."

In the parable of the rich man who had made a lot of money in agriculture, the man said to himself, I know what I will do, I will tear down my barns and build bigger ones and have food and wine to drink for the rest of my days. To which, the Lord said, "You fool! This very night your life will be demanded from you. Then who will get what you have prepared for yourself?" (See Luke 12:16-20.)

Building and creating wealth increases the size of the pie. Another way we used to say it is that the rising tide lifts all boats. Creating wealth lifts all boats. It is an important concept as opposed to buying into poverty. Poverty is a curse, not a blessing according to Deuteronomy 28:15 (NLT): "But if you refuse to listen to the Lord your God and do not obey all the commands and decrees I am giving you today, all these curses will come and overwhelm you."

There are so many verses about wealth. Being wealthy isn't the issue. It is how you acquire it and what you do with it that counts--how you respond to who God is in your life. Ask yourself, "What role does wealth play relative to my faith?" As long as it doesn't get in the way of your faith, and as long as you are ready to do whatever God calls you to do with what he has given you, wealth is not the issue.

HOWARD DAHL on
GREED (bio pp. 253-254)

Greed has no limit. Just because someone has a lot of money doesn't mean they can't be extremely greedy. I know people who feel poor because they only have a small plane and not a Gulfstream. Greed and envy don't know socio-economic boundaries.

A big part of the current economic mess is that leaders were very greedy and couldn't have cared less how their decisions affected others. I think much of the problem is the consolidated debt obligations. Most people didn't understand them. Leading agencies were either ignorant—not understanding them—or they were evil—closing their eyes and giving high ratings to instruments that were shams. I'd like to think they were ignorant and not malicious, but who knows what was in their heart.

ED MEESE on
THE ECONOMY (bio pp. 259-260)

One of my friends, a biblical scholar, said Jesus talked about money a lot in his teachings, largely along the lines of, "For where your treasure is, there your heart will be also" (Matthew 6:21). First of all, Christians cannot panic, as many people are doing now. Secondly, if Christians are saving their money, are being prudent as to how they spend their money, and not living beyond their means, they will be a positive force.

Most of the economic problems we are facing right now are due to people, businesses, and organizations living beyond their means. If there is any particular lesson, it is that. I also believe in the idea that if you give the first fruits of your earnings to the Lord, then you will be blessed. If this Christian lifestyle of handling money were a regular part of more people's lives, I don't think we would be in some of the problems that we are in today.

If you look at what has happened, most of the problems in the mortgage industry occurred because people violated their responsibilities to their businesses, made loans that were not appropriate, and neglected to follow the rules. If common sense, ordinary prudence, responsibility, and these kinds of characteristics—which should be the characteristics of every Christian life—were applied to businesses on a routine basis, we wouldn't have the magnitude of problems we are facing today.

The other thing that Christians can do is help those who are in need right now. They can help through their churches, which sometimes find temporary housing, provide assistance with childcare, or offer other services people need. Then we could meet their needs more in a spirit of friendship and camaraderie than with an attitude of giving charity.

STEVE LYNN on
GIVING AND SAVING (bio pp. 258-259)

First off, you are called to tithe—and that applies to your time, talents, and money. Secondly, don't live beyond your means—don't live off of debt. Don't live off credit cards. Third, learn to say no to good things. Oswald Chambers, in *My Utmost for His Highest*, essentially says that the enemy of being our utmost for God isn't evil. We say no to evil pretty well. But if we say "yes" to every good thing, we won't be able to be great at anything.

BONNIE and STEVE WURZBACHER on
BUSINESS AS THE ONLY CREATOR OF WEALTH
(bios on pp. 268 & 269, respectively)

Churches, schools, charities, and mission fields are voracious consumers of wealth. Successful businesses are the only creators of that wealth.

Through my Christian worldview, the role of business is to build and advance the economic well being of communities throughout the world so that each person can fulfill his or her God-given purpose. And, as the sole means of wealth creation, business makes it possible for all of society's social institutions to exist—from governments to charities.

A healthy and well-run company has vast potential to accomplish good. Translating that potential into reality requires an enabled culture of "corporate citizenship." At Coca-Cola, this culture models how we are to conduct our business in four broad areas: the marketplace, the workplace, the environment, and the community.

I am proud of The Coca-Cola Company and the good that it accomplishes in communities around the world. Our beverages are produced right in the communities where they are consumed at over eight hundred bottling plants in two hundred countries. These businesses are locally owned and controlled. When they succeed, they spawn myriad more enterprises and micro-enterprises, creating jobs and opportunities where our consumers live. These consumers account for more than 1.4 billion servings of our beverages every single day.

In return, The Coca-Cola Company and our franchisees and partners give back generously. From disaster relief to clean water initiatives to fighting AIDS on the African continent—Coke strives to be a great corporate citizen, as well as a generous benefactor. Public and private foundations, spawned by business wealth, as well as generous individual businesspeople, undergird most philanthropies and not-for-profit organizations. The taxes that support the rest are also driven by business success. The Coca-Cola Company understands that because we have been given much—starting with the loyalty of generations of consumers—much is required of us. We also understand that businesses can only be successful, in the long-term, if the communities they serve are healthy and sustainable.

Roberto Goizueta, former Chairman of Coca-Cola, expressed this idea eloquently:

> We live in a democratic, capitalist society, and here people create specific institutions to help meet specific needs. Governments are created to help meet civic needs. Philanthropies are created to help meet financial needs. Churches are created to help meet spiritual needs. And companies are created to help meet economic needs. Business distributes the lifeblood that flows through our economic system, not only in the form of goods and services, but also in the form of taxes, salaries, and philanthropy. While a healthy company can have a positive and seemingly infinite impact on others, a sick company is a drag on the social order of things. It cannot serve customers. It cannot give to philanthropic causes. And it cannot contribute anything to society.

Michael Novak in, *Business as a Calling*, expands on this reality, "This creative community (business) is, with the exception of Christianity, the greatest transforming power of the poor on earth." Business seeks out persons of talent, initiative, and enterprise who want to better their condition and that of others, and it can indeed be a high calling.

We all seek to have our daily work count toward a higher purpose and to satisfy the questions the Holy Spirit fills us with. "Am I fulfilled through the work that I am doing?" "Do I honor and glorify God in my work?" "Am I contributing toward the building of his kingdom?"

We all need meaning in our work. We need a sense that we are contributing to something larger than ourselves and as Christians, that we are serving to advance God's purposes in the world. When we recognize that God calls us to bring meaning to our vocation, and we use our gifts and talents to serve his purposes and bring glory to him, we can gain great fulfillment in our daily work.

what is your take on money?

join the conversation at
www.oursoulsatwork.com/money

Blake Mycoskie, Chief Shoe Giver and Founder of TOMS Shoes

CHAPTER SIX
STEWARDSHIP

"For what does it profit a man to gain the whole world, and forfeit his soul?"

Mark 8:36 NASB

In the business world there is an emerging social consciousness, referred to as Corporate Social Responsibility (CSR) or the triple bottom line, denoting measurable financial, social, and environmental outcomes for business. In addition to making a profit, there is increased awareness that we need to take care of one another and the environment in order for humanity to flourish.

Most people of faith are aware of their need to live and behave according to scriptural teachings. However, what is missing sometimes is the shift from thinking purely in terms of personal behavior to the collective behavior of an institution, such as a business, or of society.

In Scripture there is a pervasive principle—generally referred to as stewardship—that we are called by God to take care of what he has given us in terms of our skills, talents, finances, as well as our influence and impact on others. The workplace is a natural setting where we are able to steward those God-given resources individually and collectively.

We need to ask ourselves, "What does it mean to be a good steward in business?" With some imagination we can quickly see that business can be an instrument that empowers rather than exploits the poor, protects rather than degrades God's creation, and enables us to be all that God desires. The goal of this chapter is expand our vision and broaden our horizons for the good that business can do—and hopefully the beginning of a conviction that we are the people who can do it.

BLAKE MYCOSKIE on FOR-PROFIT PHILANTHROPY
THE SUCCESS OF TOMS SHOES (bio pp. 262-263)

I'm a serial entrepreneur, having started five companies in twelve years. In 2006, I was burnt out and traveled to Argentina to relax, explore, and soak in the culture. In the process, I met a few social workers focusing on some of the villages on the outskirts of Buenos Aires and asked if I could tag along.

In one village, I noticed most of the children didn't have shoes, and if they did, they were too small, too big, duct taped, or ancient flip-flops. It shocked me. In my experience, shoes didn't seem that expensive. My shock deepened when I examined their feet and saw cuts, infections, and infestations.

It struck me this problem should be easy to solve. The idea came to start TOMS Shoes, a company that matches every pair of shoes purchased with a pair of new shoes given to a child in need—one for one. As of August 1, 2009, TOMS has given away 150,000 pairs of shoes.

Overcoming challenges

When I got the idea for TOMS Shoes, I had absolutely no experience in the fashion or shoe industry. The businesses I had started were in the technology and media world. Nothing had prepared me for this. I'm very curious, an explorer, and when I find needs that aren't being met, I like to create businesses that meet them.

The learning curve was intense. In a short time, while I was still in Argentina, I met with shoemakers, canvas vendors, and hired interns in America. It was the hardest and the most exciting part of TOMS, starting a business in an industry I knew nothing about. It's been a wild ride, but one well worth it.

Focus on a sustainable business model

It was important to create a company that was sustainable, that would provide for others consistently. A nonprofit would have worked, but soliciting donors year after year was tenuous, if they lost interest in my charity—what then? The children would be without shoes. With a sustainable for-profit business model, TOMS is able to stick to its promise, consistently providing shoes to children in need. As long as we can produce a good product that sells, every sale means another child receives a pair of shoes.

Our customers get to be part of making a difference. They love the idea. We officially launched TOMS Shoes online and in a few Los Angeles stores on May 5, 2006. Booth Moore wrote an article about us that ran in the *Los Angeles Times* May 20, 2006, and we sold more than 2,000 pairs of shoes over the weekend! I hired three interns to take orders, and since I only had 200 pairs of shoes in my apartment, I returned to Argentina to produce more. It took three months to fill the backorders.

Giving equals success

It gives me satisfaction to know that children around the world are receiving a pair of TOMS shoes because of a simple idea I had in 2006. My parents always engaged us in community service through our church. I learned what it was like to help others and see the immediate effects of helping. When I went into business, I always wanted to incorporate giving into whatever I did, and to me, it is success to have managed to do that with TOMS. In a sense, it's allowed me to go into ministry without having to leave my passion for entrepreneurialism.

I experience a sense of success as well, when I see my employees and customers around the world join in the "One for One" movement. It's amazing to watch it grow.

TOMS has strengthened my faith. Being around the impoverished and seeing their love and joy, how happy they are with what they have, has given me inner happiness. Providing shoes and seeing how life-changing that simple act is makes me thankful for all of the gifts I have been given.

BLAKE LINGLE on
A FAITH-REFLECTIVE BUSINESS MODEL (bio p. 258)

My first business was Card Shop. I opened it in my parents' woodshed. We thrived for about two days. Shortly after we ran our first advertising campaign, a cardboard box on which we'd strategically painted "cards" and an arrow, the Boise Police shut us down for not having a business license—a crushing blow for a seven-year-old. The business did not recover. A boys-only superhero club took over the space.

My only goal for Card Shop was to sell enough cards to buy other cards. I had more goals when I started Boise Fry Company (BFC) twenty years later: making amazing fries and burgers and creating an ethical business, influenced by and representative of my relationship with Christ. The latter goal, to me, meant helping the poor, protecting the Earth, and treating people like Christ would.

Some of the poorest, most disenfranchised people in America right now are recently arrived refugees. Though the U. S. Government invites refugees to America, they are not entitled to the same government aid as Americans. Their aid ends six to eight months after arriving. Not only do they come from dire circumstances—from places like Somalia, Iraq, and Bhutan—but they're also forced into dire circumstances if they don't find a job quickly in the U. S. Unfortunately, given the current economy, finding a job is very difficult.

Providing jobs to refugees is one way BFC can help the poor. God commands us throughout the Old and New Testament to help the poor. God doesn't elaborate much on how to help; he just wants us to help. God also puts increased expectations on the rich and those in authority. I'm not a rich person—by relative American terms, anyway. I flip burgers for a living. However, as a business owner, I have the authority to provide jobs, and thereby income, to the poor. It's one way I can live out my faith.

Minimizing BFC's effect on the environment is another reflection of my faith.

There are many reasons why I feel we should protect the Earth.

- One: The Holy Spirit is here amongst us, and just like us, he doesn't like seeing his surroundings polluted. He says so in Numbers 35:34 NLT: *"You must not defile the land where you live, for I live there myself."*
- Two: Evangelism. Earth's beauty, and the fact that we can appreciate it, is often cited as a means for understanding and acknowledging God. Romans 1: 20 (NLT) says: "From the time the world was created, people have seen the earth and sky and all that God made. They can clearly see his invisible qualities—his eternal power and divine nature. So they have no excuse whatsoever for not knowing God." I want the Earth to stay as pristine as possible, so people can see God.
- Three: The Earth is not ours to keep. God is permitting us to use it. "The Earth is the Lord's, and everything in it," as it says in Psalm 24:1 (NLT). I know if God let me borrow his Pinto—I imagine God driving something humble—I would not return it with a flat. Nor do I want to return the Earth with a flat.

The hospitality industry is a big polluter, restaurants especially. Restaurants buy, make, and trash lots of products. When we started BFC, we made a decision to buy organic, sustainable, and biodegradable products, in an effort to become one of the only one hundred percent green restaurants in the United States. Some of our green products include biodegradable fry cones, napkins, and to-go cups. We also recycle some of our waste. Our excess potatoes are recycled to grow more potatoes and our used peanut oil is recycled in cars. And finally, we use Energy Star freezers and refrigerators and low-wattage, energy-efficient light bulbs. We're not fully green yet, but we're making progress.

Furthermore, a healthy Earth makes for a healthy body. Modern farming (some, not all) has extracted nutrients from food and replaced them with pesticides.

That, coupled with the preservatives added to most processed foods, makes for unhealthy meals. In my opinion, pesticides and preservatives are as much to blame for obesity as saturated fats. Organic food is devoid of the pesticides that are polluting our bodies.

At BFC, when feasible and/or affordable, we purchase local, natural, and organic foods. We also prepare everything in house, which prevents the need for preservatives. Finally, we don't adulterate our humble fare with unnecessary ingredients and fat. Potatoes and peanut oil are the only ingredients in our fries. Other fast food fries have most, if not all, of the following ingredients: potatoes, vegetable oil, partially hydrogenated soybean oil, natural beef flavor, wheat and milk derivatives, citric acid (preservative), dextrose, sodium acid pyrophosphate (maintain color), dimethylpolysiloxane (antifoaming agent), and salt. Yikes! I'm no physiological expert, but I can't imagine that some of those ingredients are good for you. As it says in 1 Corinthians 6:19, our body is a temple, and though we understand that fries and burgers aren't the healthiest foods, we strive to serve the healthiest, most amazing fries and burgers around.

We also strive for amazing service at BFC. Toward the end of the movie *Family Man*, Nicolas Cage's character says this during a job interview, "Business is business. Wall Street, Main Street, it's all a bunch of people getting up in the morning trying to figure out how . . . they're going to send their kids to college. It's just people . . . and I know people." This quote often surfaces in my mind throughout the course of a business day. I'd like to think I understand people and that my understanding of people developed from my relationship with Christ. Christ gives plenty of advice on how to deal with people.

The second great commandment is to love your neighbor as yourself, so in some sense, by some transitive property, Christ gave excellent business advice. Understanding and appreciating people, both employees and customers, is the cornerstone for most ethical, successful businesses. Our service model at BFC is based on the second great commandment.

We recognize Christ was not and is not in the business of making money. I remember that when my relationship with Christ influences my business decisions. I also like to remind myself that anything he gives us, he can take away. We shouldn't use Christ as some business pundit for the accumulation of wealth. However, as Christians within the context of our business, we can have incredible impact on those around us. From customers to vendors to employees, we interact with lots of people on any given day, some may not know or believe in Christ.

Interaction is our greatest witness. People won't attribute God to building a Fortune 500 company. People will attribute God to how you treat them. If you're involved in business, don't just sell a product to buy more products, like I did with Card Shop. We sell products because that's how we build our economy—but while selling products, we can let people see our relationship with Christ, because that's how we build the Kingdom.

JOHN TYSON on
BIO-FUELS (bio pp. 267-268)

One of the greatest debates we've got to answer in this country is the ethanol debate. Six-dollar corn is starting to harm people's ability to eat food around the world right now. When you study the science of ethanol, it does not do what it is perceived to. I do not think, long-term, it is a viable alternative. It is driving up the cost of food for poor people, not only in the United States, but also around the world. It's a feel-good story, but it's not a good economic or environmental story.

I strongly support the development of renewable fuels, but they should be produced from agricultural by-products, not from feed grains like corn that should be used to feed humans directly, or be fed to animals that will be used for the production of protein to feed people around the globe.

KIMBERLY YERINO on BUSINESS AS MINISTRY and AN ANSWER TO POVERTY (bio p. 269)

A poor man's field may produce abundant food,
but injustice sweeps it away.

Proverbs 13:23

Since childhood, I have felt called to minister to people who are in poverty. To equip me for that ministry, God led me to Yale and eventually business school. Still pursuing that path now as a corporate analyst and MBA campus minister, I find myself in an environment where my daily ministry is to a different population—the economically blessed but sometimes spiritually depleted.

The Believers in Business (BiB) Conference introduced me to marketplace ministry, a powerful theology of work and God's redeeming plan for all kinds of work—even business. Another tenet of marketplace ministry is the fundamental understanding of business as mission—seeing our work as a way God accomplishes his creative and redemptive purposes in the world.

Now I say to my business partners, students and peers, "Look at the creation story in Genesis. God made us to steward over creation, to be creative, to even find joy in subduing the chaos of a spreadsheet to produce a concise report. We reflect aspects of God's character even in that." The perspectives of marketplace ministry offer daily help to Christians called to Corporate America.

As God continued to help me understand my current daily calling as a marketplace minister, I learned about the importance of human flourishing to God. God desires for all humans to flourish by exercising their God-given creativity as established in Genesis and exemplified in Jesus.

While marketplace theology was developed in the context of Christians seeking to integrate faith and vocation in business, marketplace theology has deepened my understanding of what it means to minister to the poor. A theology of human flourishing helps illuminate the trauma of poverty and the inability to work, while adding a crucial new dimension to what it means to minister to those in that state of life.

Ministry to these families now means more to me than meeting their basic needs in the name of Jesus. It means allowing them the space to flourish in the image of God. I deeply believe that this calling is not mine alone, but for all of us on whom God has placed the spirit of leadership and the gifts of management.

It seems that our current social service paradigm treats those in poverty as "have nots." So we focus our energy on giving—food, clothing, shelter, Bibles. All of these are good and necessary, but insufficient as a holistic ministry. I first encountered a Scripture that shattered the "have nots" paradigm for me when Spencer Brand exhorted us to read one Proverb every day. I gave it a try that March. During one such devotional, I was struck by Proverbs 13:23, "A poor man's field may produce abundant food, but injustice sweeps it away."

We often envision the poor as foraging at the corners of another's field. (See Leviticus 19:9.) We do not generally see poor people as landowners. For me this proverb exploded the view that the poor are those without resources. I also began to see the "field" as a metaphor for our God-given creative capacity, or our potential to do good works, bear fruit, and flourish as human beings.

People in poverty have abundant gifts and talents, love and faith. As Proverbs 22:2 NKJV reads, "Rich and poor have this in common; The Lord is the Maker of them all." We are all endowed with creative capacity, being made in the image of God. But injustice—the lack of opportunity to use these talents and do good works—sweeps away the fulfillment and flourishing that we, as God's image bearers, enjoy from using those talents productively. Thus, those in poverty are deprived of their ability to live up to their God-given potential by unemployment, discrimination, segregation, and inequality.

The Lord has placed on my heart that as believers in the field of business, God is not only calling us to glorify him by working hard, being creative, and participating in his redeeming work at our jobs, but also to use our gifts to enable the flourishing of others. This is the ministry of business. Jeff Van Duzer, Dean of Seattle Pacific's business school has said, "Business exists in society in order to provide a platform in which people can express aspects of their God-given identity through meaningful and creative work."

At the same time, the Bible overwhelms us with exhortations to serve the needy; from Leviticus 19:9-10, "Do not reap to the very edges of your field . . . leave them for the poor," to Isaiah 58:6, 7, "Is not this the kind of fasting I have chosen . . . to share your food with the hungry and to provide the poor wanderer with shelter," to the parable of the Good Samaritan and to Matthew 25:40, "Whatever you did for one of the least of these brothers of mine, you did for me."

Nevertheless, we often think of caring for the poor in terms of gifts we give, rather than empowering them to provide for themselves and be a blessing to others. Psalm 113:7-8 states that the Lord our God "raises the poor from the dust and lifts the needy from the ash heap [and] he seats them with princes."

How is it that our social service institutions have taken those that the Lord seats with princes in Christ and has herded them like cattle to get food, violated their privacy to get housing, and denied them childcare to get jobs? The tragedy of poverty is not only the health and psychological costs of not having money, but the spiritual cost of being dehumanized to the point of forgetting that we are all made in the image of God.

Long-term unemployment has been well documented to lead to feelings of frustration, inadequacy, and lost hope. In his book, *A People's History of Poverty in America*, Stephen Pimpare quotes one lady on public assistance (pg. 196):

What do I want to be? Gosh, I don't allow myself the luxury to think of these things. It's a luxury to think of things about myself in any other way than I am now. What I have to do is survive. I can't think about what I want to be.

An unwillingness to work does not cause Americans to fall into poverty. Rather, poverty robs people of the motivation to work, or sweeps it away. Disadvantaged but otherwise hard-working Americans find themselves in an economic system that makes challenging and well-paying jobs very scarce, and in many places, non-existent.

As people made in the image of God, impoverished Americans not only find themselves debilitated by their inability to work, but further humiliated by always being the recipient of aid. Proverbs 11:25 reads, "A generous man will prosper; he who refreshes others will himself be refreshed." We have all experienced the blessing we receive from helping others. Yet often those we serve do not receive the same opportunity to receive such a blessing by helping us. Just as we are called to bring the good news of the Gospel to those who do not know Christ, the good news that we as businesspeople bring to the poor and the unemployable is that they are made in the image of God.

Several Christian and non-Christian organizations such as Habitat for Humanity and Greyston Bakery have built the dignity of work into their business models. Our task is to meditate on God's Word and see where God has gifted us to serve his people in need. Perhaps our entrepreneurial aspirations or our role as a hiring manager will create good work for others. As believers in business, our gifts position us especially well to bring this good news to those who are poor, to join the Lord in affirming the dignity of every human being as an image-bearer of God. Our jobs allow us to experience God's fingerprints and blessings on us. As Jesus exhorted us at the end of the parable of the Good Samaritan in Luke 10:30-37, so now I encourage you to "Go and do likewise."

how can we steward our talents and resources through business?

join the conversation at
www.oursoulsatwork.com/stewardship

CHAPTER SEVEN
BALANCE

"Work for six days and rest the seventh so your ox and donkey may rest and your servant and migrant workers may have time to get their needed rest."

Exodus 23:12 THE MESSAGE

A friend of mine once took a pay cut to take a job where he would be expected to work only sixty hours a week. In some industries, like investment banking, people spend as much as 100 hours a week at work. A forty-hour workweek is hard to come by for most professionals. Add in commute time and it can feel like all we do is work, work, work.

There is a very real tension of how much is too much when it comes to the time we spend working. How can we balance work with other worthy responsibilities, like a spouse and children for those who have them? Maybe there is no real balance. I once heard a speaker say, "God worked six days; that's not balance!" Point taken.

Balance is a challenging term as it implies equitable division of activity. According to that interpretation, there really can be no work-life balance *per se*; it is more like work-life *tension*. However, we are whole people so our lives have to be lived in an integrated fashion, even though there will be tension. Do I work more, or do I go home and play with the kids? Today's technology enables us to work everywhere all of the time. In my grandfather's generation, although they worked six-day workweeks, when the sun went down the workday ended. We are living in the age of connectivity when all things are possible at all times of the day. Therefore we must increasingly grapple with how we balance work with the rest of life's responsibilities.

God worked and calls us to work, but God does call mothers to be mothers, fathers to be fathers, spouses to be spouses, and all of us to study his Word, go to church, and a host of other things that require time. Jesus modeled a life of diverse activity. The biblical account shows him celebrating at a wedding, sleeping on a boat, enjoying a dinner party, and retreating for prayer. If there is anyone who could have justified working all the time, surely it was Christ.

Followers of Christ, therefore, need to reflect on all of life's priorities and ensure that we don't let life slip by and in the end, realize that we misspent God's gift of time. Our allocation of time is similar to all of the other resources we have. It needs to be spent in accordance to godly values and principles.

No one achieves the balance of life perfectly. We are all a work in progress. Most executives and entrepreneurs acknowledge balance as one of the most difficult things to achieve. Nevertheless, this chapter contains a lot of valuable insights that are worth mulling over in our quest for properly spending our time.

HENRY KAESTNER on
FOUR CORE VALUES (bio pp. 256-257)

Bandwidth.com, like any company our size, has a unique working environment. Projects get done in a particular way, communication happens in ways subtly different from other companies, and individual and teamwork patterns are unique to Bandwidth.com. In aggregate, all of this makes up our distinct corporate culture.

Three components primarily influence our culture: our values, our leadership, and our people. Of the three, our values are most important as they shape the other two.

David Morken and I want to see the same core values drive the company that drive our lives. That means we focus on faith, family, work, and fitness—in that order. We believe, if we balance all four well, and in that order, we'll be successful.

Faith
We firmly believe our success has come from God, and we work for his glory. It's impossible to spend any meaningful time with us and not know that our Christian faith is what guides and drives us. David and I don't pass out tracts at work; in

fact, people from several different faith backgrounds are part of our team. I believe everyone feels valued and not judged.

We're always ready to share why we have hope, but it's most important for us to model faith as being what we live for. It's our faith that compels us to submit our products, services, and relationships to the highest standard—a biblical standard. Even though we often fall short, we are always aiming toward that goal.

Family

I came to North Carolina from New York. While New York City doesn't have a monopoly on the seventy-hour workweek, there are few places on Earth where that value (or anti-value) is more prominently on display. I know too many families and lives that have been shattered by overwork. David and I have nine children between us, and we're all too aware we have two hours at most to be a Dad each weekday. For us, it's the hours between 6:30 to 8:30 p.m. We cherish that time with our families and want our employees to be able to as well. There are no heroics in staying in the office late at the expense of family. We all have plenty of time to get back online once we've put kids to bed. That happens most nights. The one night it won't happen is "date night"—that's when I get to take the boys' mom out to tell her how much I appreciate what she does.

Without a firm faith and family commitment, the next value just doesn't happen.

Work

David and I love our work. We like to lead; we like to create and innovate. We like to compete; we like to win. We like to challenge those who work with us, just as they challenge us. We like to question; we like to listen. We can always be better, and we love that, too. Work is the manifestation of much of who we are.

Fitness

Work hard; play hard. David and I go on a run or a bike ride just about every lunch hour when we're in town. Our employees follow our lead, and depending on the day of the week, droves of co-workers will head out for a game of ultimate

Frisbee or soccer on the fields near our office, or basketball on the campus court. Some of our best partner retreats and senior management trips have revolved around fitness. We've had epic trips to ride mountain stages during the Tour de France, surfed with our channel team in Costa Rica, and gone heli-skiing several times. Fitness, particularly when done in groups, provides some of our best camaraderie, exchange of ideas, and rest from work.

DAVID MORKEN on THE DISCIPLINE OF WORK / LIFE BALANCE AS A CEO (bio pp. 261-262)

As a CEO, I'm as busy as I want to be. It can consume all my waking and some sleeping moments, if I let it. The work can become an idol that you worship morning, noon, and night, and the pace can be absolutely invigorating and seemingly fulfilling. Over the years, it has been important to establish balance. You can only sacrifice family, your walk with Christ, and your physical health for so long before it catches up with you. Work in entrepreneurial capitalist gear, pushing the pedal to the metal for too long, will catch up with you—and you *will* explode.

I get up at 6:00 a.m. and start work no later than 8:00 a.m., often over breakfast with another leader at Bandwidth, and I'm done at 6:00 p.m. In the middle of the day, I take time for a ninety-minute workout. That's important, and I fit it in about four days a week. I try to limit travel to no more than one night a week away from the family. It has been an intentional business discipline to maintain the middle of the day workout and take only the most important trips, as well as avoiding being away from home more than one night a week. Balance has to be "on purpose."

Balance comes into play in leadership. We have a lot to accomplish, at high cost sometimes. Without the love of Christ, I could destroy the families of a lot of executives here. If I work late, they work late. If I didn't kick them out at 6:00 p.m., they'd stay and work. When you have alpha-type, hard-charging men and women working together, and they're having a blast at what they do, they could easily work too hard at the expense of their families. It's because I have a Savior that I won't let the team burn themselves out. We actually have signs reminding folks to be home in time for dinner. (See sign on pages 144-145)

When we hired our Vice President of Strategy, he shared an office with me—which he still does. He had come from a firm where he charged hard, so I had to kick him out every day at 6:00 p.m. At first, he thought he must be doing something wrong, or that we were going to dock his pay, but he's come to understand the importance of balance. Now at 6:00 p.m., you'll find him making sure his team of eighteen is on their way out the door for home.

There is never an easy time to bring balance; you always have to do it now. Understanding and respect for the importance of family and life outside work versus a sole focus on creating value in the company is the essence of our leadership. Don't get me wrong. I'm a red-blooded, American capitalist. I love to create value and serve lots of customers. I love to be relevant and deliver a fantastic customer experience at low cost, but not at the expense of our team or the integrity of the families involved in supporting Bandwidth. I think that's how we create a Christian foundation for everything we do.

DAVID MORKEN on
FITTING IN ULTRA-MARATHONS (bio pp. 261-262)

I am a confessed endurance-event addict. The first year I competed in an ultra-marathon (one hundred miles), I depended only on the ninety-minute workouts to get in shape. It wasn't enough, and I dropped out at mile seventy. The second year I was fortunate to finish. Consistently fitting in ninety minutes of running five days a week and a twenty-mile run on the weekends made the difference. The long runs needed to happen early in the morning or after the kids went to bed, because I was determined not to take time away from them. When training for the Iron Man Triathlon, I did the same except that I usually fit in a six-hour bike ride on the weekend. Even while training for a major endurance event, I guard my time with family.

DAVID MORKEN on
ESTABLISHING AND MAINTAINING
THE DISCIPLINE OF FAMILY TIMES (bio pp. 261-262)

My wife and I have six children ranging in age from four to sixteen, three boys and three girls. Early on, Chrishelle and I chose to establish certain disciplines to support our values as a family. For example, dinner as a family is very important to all of us. Even though our children are in football, soccer, and other activities, we wait for everyone to get home and eat together, usually at least four times a week, and reserve one weekend evening (leaving one for sleepovers, etc.) to share as a family.

In the evenings, I am one hundred percent Dad until bedtime. This is non-negotiable.

Being assistant coach for my sons' Pop Warner football team helps me stay connected individually with my sons. Between time on the field and driving to and from practice and games, we have been able to have great conversations and deepen our bond through the shared activities. My daughters play soccer. Saturdays usually find me on the field cheering them on. We are a part of our children's lives, and we wouldn't have it any other way.

Vacations and holidays are family affairs, too. We love to camp, backpack, fish, and climb mountains. We spend a lot of time in tents and enjoying the outdoors. For the first fourteen years of our marriage, there wasn't a night when both of us were away from our children, not because it was a rule, but because we simply enjoy our family that much. We'd rather be together.

One great activity our whole family loves is reading together. Books by C.S. Lewis, J.R.R. Tolkien, and Christian missionary biographies are favorites with our kids. They often make an extra effort to be home for our reading time.

Live Well

Faith and Family first....Take time to recharge....Minimize Travel....Be home for dinner as much as possible

INTUITIVE VOICE, INTERNET & APPS

DELIVERED BY A SINGLE TRUSTED PARTNER

AT AN EXCEPT

Lynn D'Eracole
is a great mom to her boys

Lynn is an example of one of the many great parents at our company.
She puts her family first and builds her schedule around their schedules.

THE CAPACITY TO BE GREAT

PRODUCTIVITY

AS-A-SERVICE

#8

... be home for dinner

I can't say enough positive things about my bride of seventeen years. She is amazing. Although, Chrishelle and I don't have a "date night" practice, most evenings find us relaxing together and talking over the day after the kids are in bed. It's so intense with six children and the business—which can seem like a seventh, special needs child—every waking moment. We need to check the pulse on our relationship and each other's well-being. We're under so much logistical and time pressure, we can't afford to drift apart. Over this time we've learned to communicate with key words and phrases and accomplish quite a bit even in a brief exchange.

STEVE REINEMUND on
WORK / LIFE BALANCE (bio p. 264)

Work/life balance has been a struggle throughout my career. My decision to retire (as CEO of PepsiCo) centered on that issue. At the time, I had two thirteen year-olds entering high school. My wife and I decided they needed a full-time father and not a part-time one. When my older children were in high school, I had a different job with different requirements, and I was able to be a full-time father. But it is a continuing battle. It is a challenge to constantly be in the game of keeping balance in your life. And you are often going to feel you don't have it.

One of the greatest examples we can set for our children is to establish that balance. It's not healthy for kids not to work, and it is not healthy for us, as parents, to work all of the time. How do we achieve balance? How do we succeed? How do we fulfill the calling we have been given and still be good husbands and wives and parents? It's the biggest challenge out there. I hope you'll find lifelong partners that will help you through it and hold you accountable. That is certainly my case. The best help I have gotten is from these very people.

SCOTT HARRISON on
WORK / LIFE BALANCE (bio p. 256)

For three years, we've been in all-out start-up mode, which requires incredible amounts of energy. But the difference of success with social change organization like charity: water is that, instead of getting rich, we give away all the money we raise. It's the results that motivate us to keep going. We can either raise the money for fifty wells and see fifty communities receive water, or we can sit on our butts playing video games and fifty communities won't get wells. The tendency is definitely to work too hard.

I have to work hard to stay plugged into church and my community, which is challenging. I've been on fifty-three planes in the past eight months. My personal relationship with Christ is the most important thing in my life, and making sure I carve out time for that is crucial for me.

STEVE LYNN on
LIFE MODELS (bio pp. 258-259)

People ask how I learned to build a happy family when my childhood was so dysfunctional. The answer is: God heals. My early upbringing was absolutely sensational. My parents were very open about their love and happy marriage. This was a very healthy thing for a child to see. They were a handsome couple and very committed to each other. I saw and experienced that until I was about twelve when my father became an alcoholic. That's when our family started to become dysfunctional.

Fortunately, by that time I had other influences in my life. Many role models and families through the years adopted me. For example, during my junior and senior year in high school, I lived with my best friend and his family more than I lived at home. I am grateful for all who modeled for me what proper parenting and marriage look like.

WENDY MURPHY on
BALANCING ROLES AS A WOMAN (bio p. 262)

I went to the Stony Brooks School, a Christian boarding prep school, for four years. Their motto was "character before career." That has stayed with me.

It's a constant challenge to charge hard at work and walk through the door at home instantly ready to take on the roles of wife/mother/daughter. I have a wonderful husband who helps me take a step back, debrief, and chill-out when I get home. Sometimes he has to ask me to "step away from the Blackberry," but I also use the drive time to and from work to debrief the day on the phone with someone or just think it through so I can walk in the door and be somewhat sane.

It's not easy. Unplugging is especially challenging these days since we can be plugged into work just about anywhere. I can go on vacation, but the challenge is to leave work behind—not give into the urge to check my e-mails or check in using my cell phone. It will always be a battle. We just have to keep work and home balanced. It's encouraging to see that the next generation seems to have a better grasp on implementing work/life balance than ours has had.

KEN ELDRED on
THE MYTH THAT CHRISTIANS MUST BE
THE LAST ONES OUT THE DOOR (bio p. 254)

A myth of conventional wisdom is that the serious Christian is somebody who will work significant hours—always going the extra mile, if you will. How can we truly be committed to our work and only work a forty-hour week?

When we were starting the computer supplies company, I was rather new in my faith. At a church retreat, I saw a verse on the logo of the Presbyterian Life Insurance Company: "If any provide not for his own, and specially for those of his own house, he hath denied the faith, and is worse than an infidel." (1 Timothy

5:8 KJV) It struck me as interesting. God is saying that we are supposed to take care of our family. I realized right there that he must have some set of priorities we should all be following. I wondered if there were others. As I searched, I stumbled on another verse dealing with priorities: "Seek ye first the kingdom of God, and his righteousness; and all these things shall be added unto you" (Matthew 6:33 KJV). The word "all" is not a limited word; the dictionary says it means "everything."

According to the Bible, setting proper priorities means putting God first—"Seek ye first the kingdom of God." That this should be our first priority is made clear. The verse from First Timothy above made me think that a close second is family, which means spouse and children. I interpreted "providing for" as encompassing all the needs of my family, including quality time, attention, relationship, and fun. After those foundational requirements are met, work—as in generating income—becomes a priority.

As a good MBA, I asked myself, "Okay, if these are the objectives, how much time do I need to spend with God every day? To build a better relationship with him? To love him more? To understand him more? How much time do I need to spend with my wife and children? What about my personal needs for rest and exercise?" I wrote down what was a reasonable amount of time for each of my priorities and added up the hours they would take during a five-day workweek. I put in eight hours for sleep a day. Then, subtracting the total from the number of hours in five days, I came up with basically forty hours a week left to do my work. It was clear that I could only be a forty-hour-a-week kind of guy in order to keep my priorities straight.

This choice had a couple of ramifications.

First, I realized venture capitalists expect you to put in anywhere from sixty to eighty hours a week. I talked to a couple who thought the idea of starting a business on forty hours a week was nutty. They didn't want any part of it. They didn't ask how many hours I would put in, but I answered before they asked.

The response was always the same: eyes glazed over as I heard something like, "Thank you for coming in to see us. Good bye." Without venture money, what were we going to do? We ended up borrowing from our families. Our plea came with the advice, "We don't really want you to invest because this is too risky." But you know how mothers are. Mine put some money into our company. I thought she was crazy, but she said, "I believe in you." We ended up with roughly $50,000 to start our venture. My contribution was $5,000 and a grocery bag of electronic parts.

Second, I had to decide what was important. When you have lots of venture capital, sometimes hundreds of millions of dollars, priorities are not as vital. Without a lot of money, you have to be careful. "What can I do to reduce the risk? What can I afford to do—and what can I afford not to do?" Defining our limitations meant that we had to think very carefully about who we wanted to be as a business.

Each workday was very intense because I only had a few hours to do it in. I had to learn how to delegate. I doled out responsibilities, "You are going to do shipping, and you're going to do ordering and accounting. You are going to manage receiving." My staff finally looked at me and asked, "Well what are you going to do?" I told them that I was going to write the next catalog because that was our future. If the catalog drove the business, the other things just had to follow along. The result was that we had more "sweat" equity in the company, and we had more committed employees who really took ownership in the business.

RICK SCHNEIDER on
THE SABBATH (bio on pp. 255-256)

David, one of my older brothers, prepares for the beginning of his Sabbath by putting a piece of tape over the button on the door inside of his refrigerator. That way, as he celebrates his Jewish Sabbath on Friday evenings and Saturdays, he won't be turning on the light inside the refrigerator (which would count as doing work) whenever he gets something to eat. In that way, he can obey his understanding of what it means to rest on the Sabbath and still feed himself. When I first heard that, it made me wonder, "Is that really what keeping the Sabbath is all about?"

The first couple of verses in Genesis 2 punctuate the phenomenal story of the creation of everything, from the start of the universe to the appearance of the first man and first woman. Verses two and three say: "By the seventh day, God completed his work which he had done, and he rested on the seventh day from all of his work he had done. Then God blessed the seventh day and sanctified it, because in it he rested from all his work which God had created and made" (NASB).

In this very first instance of the great rest of the Sabbath, we see that God is immensely potent, extremely powerful, completely capable, incredibly creative, and yet he still rested on the seventh day. He stopped everything. Not only that, but that day is sanctified because he rested. This is one of the very first biblical principles that we are given: It's important to rest in the context of doing amazing work.

The next mention of the Sabbath is in Exodus 16. It says the people gathered twice as much bread on the sixth day so that they wouldn't have to gather any on the Sabbath. The bread here is called manna, which God was providing from heaven every morning, except on the seventh day. So the very first experience the people of Israel have with this idea of Sabbath is in the context of God's provision for them. The people of Israel knew they were only supposed to pick up enough manna to eat for each day. Anything extra would rot. But on the sixth day, they were told to pick a double helping of manna, which would still be good to eat the next day. So this picture of the Sabbath is about preparing for the day of rest—actually, receiving a double helping of provisions one day so the people can rest the next.

The next time the Sabbath appears in Scripture, it expands into something even bigger. Exodus 20 *commands* us to keep the Sabbath holy. In Exodus 23, the Sabbath is extended to cover one of the primary factors of production: the land. Land is the most important part of the Israelites' existence because God's promise to them was connected to the land. The land itself is to be given a special rest every seven years, as if somehow it reflects some great principle of what God, who created the universe, is all about.

In Exodus 31, the Sabbath is given a special ceremonial role. The Sabbath is set aside to publicize something very special that the Lord has done. The sons of Israel shall observe the Sabbath and celebrate the Sabbath throughout the generations as a sign of their perpetual covenant with God. So the Sabbath is not just for an experience God has made important. It is also for publicizing something important about the nature of God and his provision for us.

Then Jesus comes and makes a new covenant. He gives new and very special teachings about the Sabbath. In Mark 6:31, Jesus says to his disciples, "Come with me by yourselves to a quiet place and get some rest." He gives this gentle command to his disciples after they returned from doing great works with God. He sent them out two by two, and they saw amazing things happen. They came back practically skipping, giving these reports of what God had done and surging with this great sense of victory. Something important is happening as humans choose to work alongside God in this kingdom work. So Jesus takes them aside to get physical rest. Or at least he tries to.

Matthew 11:28-30 describes the kind of rest that Jesus cared about providing for all of his children: "Come to me, all you who are weary and burdened, and I will give you rest. Take my yoke upon you and learn from me, for I am gentle and humble in heart, and you will find rest for your souls. For my yoke is easy and my burden is light." Jesus demonstrates his concern for bodily rest as well as for rest of the heart and soul. He has publicized an important element of the Sabbath that should have never been forgotten.

In Mark 2:27-28, Jesus was criticized for healing someone on the Sabbath. Jesus responds this way: "The Sabbath was made for man, not man for the Sabbath. So the Son of Man is Lord even of the Sabbath." Instead of declaring an end to the practice of observing the Sabbath, Jesus says he is now "Lord of the Sabbath." He wants to free his people from the oppressive conditions that had been attached to the Sabbath by the religious leaders. People were working so hard to keep all the rules that the true purpose of the Sabbath had been lost. Instead, Jesus taught that as Lord of the Sabbath he came to give rest for the body as well as the soul.

What does that mean for us now? What does that mean for faith at work?

First of all, Jesus frees us from the oppression of rituals. None of us have to actually put tape on the refrigerator door's light button. I grow sad when I hear my brother talk about practicing this specific ritual, and I grow even sadder when I read the Bible passages that make it clear the Sabbath is supposed to be something enlivening and life-giving for us. The first step is to understand that we are freed from rituals.

Second, Jesus frees us from frenzy. The word "Sabbath" comes from the Hebrew word *Shabbat*, which simply means "to cease." Even in those first chapters of the Bible where we are told the Lord is resting, the point is he *ceased* from his labor, not that he grew tired and therefore needed to rest—but that he decided to cease from his labor for his own reasons. We need to remember that the Sabbath is given to us as a reminder that it is actually okay to cease from our labors long enough to be renewed and refreshed.

Take a day to cease from the frenzy of an economy in crisis. For a moment, rest in dependence upon God. This is a key element of the Sabbath that I didn't realize during much of my life. It's not simply structured to remind us that God is the most important thing in our lives. It's a time when we can rest and remember that our sustenance is provided for, just like the manna that God gave the Israelites from heaven. That's the primary meaning behind the idea of the Sabbath.

Psalm 46:10-11 says, "Cease striving and know that I am God; I will be exalted among the nations, I will be exalted in the earth. The Lord of hosts is with us; The God of Jacob is our stronghold. Selah." (NASB) We can rest. We can cease striving and receive wisdom and blessings from God. Sabbath equals "contentment." It's a time for me to celebrate the blessing of contentment.

What does it mean to truly live the Sabbath? I often spend Sundays trying to live up to some idea of Sabbath yet never understanding what the heart of Sabbath actually is. That's because I have this "I must do—" compulsion. So now when my type-A personality pipes up with the nagging question of, "What do I have to do today?" or "What do I have to do to make that project work?" on a Sunday, I know I need to experience the discipline of the Sabbath by answering with, "Nothing."

"Nothing" in order to succeed financially or to make sure my children have a roof over their heads, enough food to eat, or are able to do the things that they like to do. I need do nothing. The only thing I need to do is remember that I am completely provided for. The discipline of the Sabbath begins for me on Sunday when I am driving to church and remembering, "Oh, that's right, this is a day when I need to do nothing, because God will provide for me."

My brother Bill, who led me to the Lord after my freshman year at Harvard, later stepped away from his faith. I eventually asked him, "Why? What's better about where you are now than where you used to be?" He answered, "I don't feel so driven anymore." He had transferred my family's compulsion to accomplish things from his professional life to his spiritual life. He also had a little voice in the back of his head always asking, "What must you do now? What must you do now?" Maybe the "must" was something noble, but even something good could become something damaging. I know one difficulty he faced was when his local church fell apart. He had poured all of his heart and soul into the building. Once it was gone, he didn't feel driven any more.

Once we are no longer under the compulsion of the world around us, we can experience Sabbath moments. You can experience contentment and freedom once you remember the Sabbath is a sense of resting in the goodness of God and his provision for you. You can even rest in the midst of an economic crisis, when you open the newspaper and wonder, "Gee, will my house soon be in one of those foreclosure articles?" Sabbath reminds me that I am being provided for, house or no house, so I can rest.

how do you balance life?

**join the conversation at
www.oursoulsatwork.com/balance**

CHAPTER EIGHT
DISCIPLINES

"Everyone who competes in the games goes into strict training. They do it to get a crown that will not last; but we do it to get a crown that will last forever."

1 Corinthians 9:25

My friend, Aaron Coleman likes to say, "All good things in life require simple disciplines." Living our faith in the marketplace is no different. Nothing of value in life comes easily, and generally requires long-term progress in the same direction. That is how spiritual disciplines, such as prayer, Bible reading, and fellowship, help us. They keep us moving toward the goal of serving and loving God and neighbor.

There is the old adage, "The more things change; the more they stay the same." We are definitely living in times of change in terms of technology, the economy, etc. . . . Yet much of life still comes down to basic fundamental principles and having the discipline to live by them. For example, there is really only one way to lose weight: burn more calories than you consume. There is only one way to avoid debt: earn more than you spend.

People tend to make these things a lot more complicated than they truly are. Frequently I go through this process: I read a book, ponder a thought, attend a series of meetings, and emerge with an answer that I already knew. Sometimes we just need to be reminded of what we have previously learned and remember to do what we already know we need to do.

The basics are the building blocks of life. Reviewing the spiritual disciplines can sometimes seem like going to Sunday school as a child again: read your Bible, pray, etc.... But due to their innate obviousness, they can elude us.

Furthermore, the basics can be hard work, which is another reason we don't always do them. Success in every area requires some hard work, however, as the verse above from Corinthians illustrates.

The stories contained in this chapter will hopefully serve to remind you of the importance of maintaining the spiritual disciplines and encourage you to take them seriously in integrating them into your daily life. They have reminded me. When I forget, I'll read this chapter again.

KEN ELDRED on
PRAYING FOR BUSINESS (bio p. 254)

There is a prevalent myth that it's not spiritual to ask for specifics in prayer, especially in business. A friend of mine is a great example of this. He managed a small contracting group and had a measure of faith. It was fairly limited, but not unusual compared to a lot of business people who say, "I do pray, but I never pray about specifics. I pray that God's will be done and I pray that God will give me wisdom and strength and guidance." Conventional wisdom says that we pray about our spouse, our kids, people in the hospital, other folks, or our nation, but not about business. We don't want to pray about *that*.

I don't know what I would have done if God had not given us those $7,000 days (see the story in chapter one on "Calling"). We ended up depending upon God. So, I asked this guy, "What do you want from God?" He said, "We just aren't as busy as we need to be, and I am having struggles keeping my people employed. I am working on getting jobs, but I can't seem to close them." I asked, "Have you prayed about what you want and what you need?" He had not.

Right there we prayed together for God to help him close sales deals and help him prosper. I did not see him for a year. When I ran into him a year ago, I asked how things were going. He said, "Ken, you aren't going to believe this. I had been praying that prayer, but I have stopped. I have so much business; I don't know what to do with it. I can't keep enough people to keep up with the deals!"

What are you praying about? God says take *everything* to him in prayer. (See Philippians 4:6). We should take everything, everything to God. Business is not excluded. He is able to do well beyond whatever we expect.

ED MEESE on
FAITH IN POLITICS (bio pp. 259-260)

Many people ask, "Can a Christian really go into politics without compromising their values and faith?" The answer is clearly, "Yes." There are a number of politicians who are great examples, and Ronald Reagan is among the best. In the thirty years that I worked for Mr. Reagan, there was never a time when I was asked to do anything that conflicted at all with my ethical principles, my religious faith, or my religious ideals; rather, I was challenged, encouraged, and reminded to utilize religious principles as a basis for decisions, actions, and particularly how we treated people. Others have asked me whether it was difficult to maintain religious principles in my jobs in government as well as in business. The answer is clearly, "No." Sometimes you had to think very carefully about what you were going to do, but I never found a time where religious beliefs and religious principles were hindrances; rather, they were great foundations for what I needed to do. I have seen this elsewhere in Washington, DC, as well, not just in the White House.

STEVE LYNN on
ACCOUNTABILITY (bio pp. 258-259)

People frequently say that we need others to hold us accountable. I see it a little differently. When I go into a new venue, I try to be transparent about my faith and values in a non-offensive way. This sets the bar of expectations for how I will conduct myself. This then allows me to use others to hold *myself* accountable.

HARRI SUNDVIK on
SPIRITUAL DISCIPLINES (bio p. 267)

I don't walk out the door of my house unless I've taken some time to be with the Lord, it's as simple as that. It is the most important appointment of every day. When I wake up at 5:30 in the morning, I'm tired, but I think about the things that are critical. Every day I pray for:

- Wisdom—the Bible promises that anyone who asks will be given wisdom. (See James 1:5).
- Love and respect—there are always smart people who don't even say hello to folks. It upsets me. In terms of team behavior, love and respect are key practices.
- Strength—which is one of the reasons I run marathons (fifty-three to date). I also pray for strength mentally, physically, and spiritually.
- Encouragement—we need to pray about this so we know how to encourage and support people yet simultaneously deal with issues that people have.
- Words—I pray for the words that are going through my mind as well as everything I write, including my e-mails. I don't pray for an hour before I send an e-mail, but I do take time to pray at the beginning of the day about such things. This is a tricky one, because you are doing a million things, multi-tasking, and suddenly you send an e-mail and when you look at it afterwards, you realize it wasn't particularly smart. Pray about your e-mails. It will save you from a lot of trouble.

Those are a few of the categories I cover in prayer each morning. Think about it and develop your own key categories. If you take the time every morning—even just five, ten, or fifteen minutes—it will make a difference in your life.

Bible reading
If you can read a one-year Bible, that's fantastic. However, it doesn't really matter as long as you have some time with God's Word. A few months ago, I wanted

to meditate and memorize some Psalms. I've written down whole Psalms on small cards, which I have with me wherever I go. I just take one verse each morning, think about it, and pray about it. You don't need to read the whole Bible as much as you need to have time in the Word. The temptation is to set the ambition level too high, become overwhelmed, and not read it all. It doesn't matter; one verse, each morning is good enough.

WENDY MURPHY on
RELIANCE ON GOD (bio p. 262)

Reliance on God is biblical, but the whole business/production system teaches reliance on self. Every time I think I'm great, I get knocked right off my chair. I'm competitive. I love to win. A humble pill I swallow every day is recognizing that without God I can do nothing. I know this, but it's a struggle. It's one reason why I read the Word every day.

When I pray, I use that old acronym ACTS (adoration, confession, thanksgiving, and supplication). It really helps me. I praise God for who he is and what he has done for us every morning and ask him to be with me all day, then read a verse and my daily devotional.

The one thing I've been struck with recently is that the Lord controls time. As leaders, one of the biggest challenges is to prioritize our time. When you're spending time with the Lord and getting energy from Him, you can go the distance. As practical people, we have so much to do, but actually we don't have to worry if we're doing what we are supposed to be doing. As we spend time with the Lord, we are better able to discern what that is and recognize that it is God who controls time—not us.

WENDY MURPHY on
BEING SALT AND LIGHT (bio p. 262)

The principle of being salt and light challenges me. It's so powerful. The market-place is dark. It's a huge challenge to be salt and light in the right way. It doesn't mean that we must go out and evangelize, but we are to shed light.

I often start my conversations with people around purpose. When someone is talking about an opportunity, sometimes I'll just ask, "How does it fit into your purpose?" Sometimes I get the chance to ask, "Do you know what your purpose is?" and that leads to very interesting conversations. It's exciting because some-times I find out somebody loves the Lord like I do. There are other times when it just gives a person something to think about. That is what we are called to do—give people something to think about.

STEVE REINEMUND on
SCRIPTURE MEMORIZATION (bio p. 264)

Memorization is not something I really thought much about, but recently a friend challenged me, and for the last six months, we have been memorizing the book of James. Every Saturday, we get on the phone and recite it to each other. We are almost done with James, and I have a new understanding of the book. I have read James many times, but it never meant anything to me like it does today.

MATTHEW McCREIGHT on
SUGGESTIONS for PERSONAL GROWTH (bio p. 259)

In my life I have developed three components to personal spiritual growth. First, I work on my faith every day. In the business world, as a Christian, we have a different operating system. Unless we work on it every day, the world will crowd it out, and when we need it, it won't be there. For me it's a discipline that really makes a difference. Find ways to work on your faith every day that fits you. Second, it's important to have a church and a community of believers. We need the help, and they need us. None of us can do this alone. That's why Hebrews says not to neglect meeting together. (See Hebrews 10:23-25.) At first, we had a tough time finding a church. We looked a long time, and finally found a wonderful, caring, faithful, intelligent place to worship at St. John's Episcopal in New Haven. It has been a tremendous thing for me to be part of community of such faithful people.

Third, we need to think about what our treasures are. For me, it's about how I balance work, family life, and faith. What will you do with your riches? What will you do with your talents? What do you treasure? I can't tell you what your riches and talents are, but it's important for you to think about your treasures. There will be ups and downs, but these three disciplines will help you get through.

FONNY SURYA on
OBEDIENCE (bio p. 267)

> *"Seek first the kingdom of God and His righteousness, and all these things shall be added to you."*
>
> *Matthew 6:33 NKJV*

It was back in 2003 when I first came to know God. I was living the dream of everyone coming from a country like Indonesia—earning U.S. dollars and working my way up the ladder in corporate America. At the peak of my career, right after my promotion, I fasted and asked God what he wanted me to do with my life. I felt very strongly God wanted me to go back home, leaving all that I had built in U.S.

It was really hard to leave all that I'd accomplished for something so vague. I always planned everything out, and God suddenly asked me to take a big leap of faith. However, I believe that God wanted me to obey—and Matthew 6:33 was my guidance. I went back home to Indonesia in 2004 and shortly after that experienced a real roller coaster ride. I continued to hold on to the fact that I did it all because I had chosen to obey God. My only hope was that God would never fail me when I acted out of obedience.

I now realize that through the roller-coaster experience, God actually brought me into a series of events that widened my exposures and shaped my maturity, which eventually helped me get into the Wharton MBA Program. It was those experiences that also brought me to my current career. Looking back, it was that one step of faith and obedience—letting go of a dream and pursuing my ambition for God—that led to the unfolding of a new and better chapter. I gave up a career only to gain a lot more.

After I graduated from Wharton, things were difficult in the credit market. My offer with one of the investment banks got rescinded because the bank was purchased. Common sense was for me to stay in New York and find a new job, which would not be easy, but still very possible given my credentials. Again, I prayed and God somehow told me that I should go back to Indonesia.

Amazingly, the investment banks back home were doing much better than those in the U.S. I actually had a chance to get involved in a couple of transactions where I was able to play a very crucial role until they closed, while my other friends were merely pitching for work. My Christian group leader once e-mailed me, "I am thinking about you and what God has done for you. He got you out of Wall Street just in time."

Throughout my life, I have never done anything overtly wrong. I don't lie. I forgive people. I tithe (or at least try to). I respect my parents and all of the other things my pastor teaches us to do. However, I know that God wants more, because most non-Christians do those things.

Obedience is very important to God. It is a further step in trusting our lives into God's hands, letting him and his plan take precedence over our own ambitions. It is a way that opens new blessings we would never have thought of before. However, our focus should not be on the blessings. We obey God because God has first loved us and sacrificed himself for us. Obedience is then a response—an act of faith in loving and giving ourselves to God.

Pray and God will reveal his plan to you. Obey and he will bring to pass all that he has in store for you. When I obey God, he never fails me.

KATHERINE FOO on
THE GOD OF PEACE AND HOPE (bio pp. 254-255)

The advent of the New Year brings hope and expectation, and brims with promise—it also brings with it, however, its share of anxiety over meeting new recruiting quotas.

No matter what, in everything, in every circumstance, I seek to hold onto the truth that God is the God of peace. He will sustain and uplift us always. It helps me to remember that the Apostle Paul wrote the following from prison:

> *Rejoice in the Lord always. I will say it again: Rejoice! Let your gentleness be evident to all. The Lord is near. Do not be anxious about anything, but in everything, by prayer and petition, with thanksgiving, present your requests to God. And the peace of God, which transcends all understanding, will guard your hearts and your minds in Christ Jesus. Finally, brothers, whatever is true, whatever is noble, whatever is right, whatever is pure, whatever is lovely, whatever is admirable—if anything is excellent or praiseworthy—think about such things. Whatever you have learned or received or heard from me, or seen in me—put it into practice. And the God of peace will be with you.*
>
> *Philippians 4:4-9*

From prison, Paul exhorted his fellow Christians to rejoice in the Lord always. He knew how to access true joy and true peace. How did he do it?

Ponder praiseworthy things

I love this reminder to think about what is true, noble, right, and pure—all that is excellent. Our thoughts influence our feelings and actions tremendously. Whenever it seems like I'm entering a spiral of anxious thoughts, I meditate on what is good, considering the beauty of the swirling snowflakes or reflecting upon a meaningful Bible verse. Doing so helps put things into perspective rather quickly.

Scripture memorization has a high return on investment. Many years back, a group of friends and I took up the challenge of memorizing the entire book of Philippians. While I've forgotten major chunks since then, I remember experiencing such a deep intimacy, joy, and contentment whenever I thought about that passage. Philippians, especially, is a wonderful book to contemplate as we go through the rigors of life.

Practice

There is some effort involved in cultivating our spiritual growth, but the rewards are far greater. In time, we will become more attuned to God's voice, and have a closer understanding of him.

The outcome is a peace that transcends all understanding from the God of peace who is always with us! I love the phrase how peace will "guard your hearts and minds"—I imagine peace standing vigilantly beside me and protecting me from anxiety. God's peace is also completely unlike the peace that this world offers. It remains unwavering and staunch in the face of all circumstances.

Refresh others

Proverb 11:25 says, "A generous man will prosper; he who refreshes others will himself be refreshed." To take our eyes off ourselves and to provide support and encouragement for others is wonderful and liberating. It helps us have a healthier perspective of life and to better understand the heart of God. As I was growing up and sharing my idealistic notions of the world with my dad, He would often tell me that I needed to help myself first before helping others. I do see the rationale behind that, but I'd venture to say that even at times when we are weary, reaching out to others could very well bless us with renewed energy and focus.

Perseverance

Perseverance is normally only seen as a necessity to weather difficult times. However, it is relevant for all parts of our lives, even when things seem to be going quite well.

Check out Hebrews 12:1-3:

> *Since we are surrounded by such a great cloud of witnesses, let us throw off everything that hinders and the sin that so easily entangles, and let us run with perseverance the race marked out for us. Let us fix our eyes on Jesus, the author and perfecter of our faith, who for the joy set before him endured the cross, scorning its shame, and sat down at the right hand of the throne of God. Consider him who endured such opposition from sinful men, so that you will not grow weary and lose heart.*

The passage indicates that we need to run this entire race set before us with perseverance, so it's not just about withstanding the hard times. It's also about keeping the right attitude and perspective, not growing tired of doing good (see Galatians 6:9), choosing daily to trust in God and praise him, etc. How do we not grow weary and lose heart?

- **Throw off the baggage of sin.** When runners participate in a race, whether a 5K or a marathon, they will keep everything as lightweight as possible. After running the Philly half-marathon, I can vouch for this! Life is an even longer journey, all the more reason to get rid of deadweight! Obstacles and sin can be vexing and insidious—once we try to cast them off, they seem to reappear and trip us up—unless we deal with the root causes. It's important to actively resist sin and repent of it, and to ask for God's grace in this matter.

- **Put on Christ.** For us, Christ endured the ultimate scorn and died a shameful death. He knew what his purpose was, and the joy set before him motivated him to keep on going. Just as Paul urged us in Philippians to consider Christ's humility so we could be humbled, let us consider how Christ endured so we can endure. He understands what we are going through. He himself was tempted. He knows that sometimes we want to give up. No matter what, we can be encouraged by his example to hold on. He will sustain us.

- **Think of the benefits.** There are various Bible verses that highlight the benefits of perseverance. Two of my favorites are:

> *We also rejoice in our sufferings, because we know that suffering produces perseverance; perseverance, character; and character, hope. And hope does not disappoint us, because God has poured out his love into our hearts by the Holy Spirit, whom he has given us.*
>
> *Romans 5:3-5*

> *Blessed is the man who perseveres under trial, because when he has stood the test, he will receive the crown of life that God has promised to those who love him.*
>
> *James 1:12*

By persevering, we'll be able to develop a stronger character, enjoy a hope that doesn't disappoint, and receive from the source of life itself! We are co-heirs with Jesus, who sat down at the right hand of the throne of God after enduring the cross. What amazing promises God gives to those who persevere. If we allow him to work powerfully in us, our hearts and minds will be changed to be more like his. Our character will be refined and we will experience the fullness of joy and hope found only in him.

BONITA GRUBBS on
GOD'S GUIDANCE (bio on pp. 255-256)

Often we do not understand how and why we are being moved to a better place. Though we might be aware that we are being led to a godly place of service, we don't have a roadmap. Romans 8:28, "we know that in all things God works for the good of those who love him, who have been called according to his purpose," serves as a reminder that things will eventually work out. The most positive results will materialize.

Challenges will come and we have to make decisions as to our course of action. Questions like, "Do I go, or do I not go?" have to be answered. The proven way is to consult God for guidance and believe that God will give it. That is what God is about, giving guidance. Sometimes it's not what we want, but God gives us the guidance for what is best in the long run.

I have learned that God can lead us to a place we don't immediately understand. One day while in my car, I clearly heard: "You are going to Yale to get your master's in public health." The radio was not on. There was no one in the car. But I clearly heard that sentence.

I replied, "But Lord, I don't want to do that. I don't want to go to Yale. I don't want to go to graduate school, especially the school of public health."

Nevertheless, I proceeded and bargained with God saying, "God, if you are behind this, and I get in, I will enroll." Not only was I accepted, but I also received master's degrees in both public health and religion.

In fact, everything I have done in twenty-two years of ministry has been something that I didn't want to do, initially. After I graduated from Yale, I didn't want to work as an administrator in the Connecticut Department of Mental Health. Yet that job helped me develop administrative and fiscal managerial skills and offered me a valuable understanding of state government. Working in the state agency led me to ordination because I understood I was looking for a calling, not just a job. I wanted to integrate my vocational desire with my faith.

I have the good fortune—although sometimes it might be described as a misfortune—to hold two masters degrees. When I was at the Divinity School, people would say to me, "Why do you want a public health degree?" When I was at the Public Health School, people would say, "Why do you want a divinity degree? What do you think that you are going to get from the two?"

For one thing, I gained a way of looking at society and why things happen in the context of a community. I learned how to look at health from a holistic view of the environment and many other viewpoints, not just from the medical side of the fence. After my first semester in public health, I was disappointed. I knew that I needed a theological anchor. That cry is what led me to the Divinity School. I knew I couldn't do this without God's help. I couldn't think about physical, psychological, and spiritual wholeness without that kind of training.

In any profession, people need to have a touchstone, to be grounded ethically and spiritually. Without that we don't have a frame of reference. That is what the two degrees allowed me to do, despite the fact that people didn't understand what I was doing and I walked alone a lot of the time. It was rather liberating to "live in two worlds," because I could carve out the path that God had laid for me.

how have spiritual disciplines affected your walk with Christ?

join the conversation at www.oursoulsatwork.com/disciplines

CHAPTER NINE
RELATIONSHIPS

"Let us consider how we may spur one another on toward love and good deeds. Let us not give up meeting together, as some are in the habit of doing, but let us encourage one another."

Hebrews 10:24-25

One of the great travesties of original sin is what it did to our relationships. As soon as God confronted Adam and Eve about who ate what, Adam started to point the finger at Eve. Shortly thereafter we read of Cain killing Abel and after that it only got worse. We humans have had a hard time with relationships ever since.

When I talk with people who are struggling in their faith, they frequently communicate that they feel as if no one understands them. When I talk to people who are strong in their faith, they frequently point to a group of close-knit relationships they have developed as the key to their success. Without relationships, we feel isolated and alone. With negative relationships, we are pulled away from what is noble and worthy. With positive relationships, we prosper and become the better for it.

We were created to be in relationship—to be in community with one another. Consistently throughout the Scriptures you see the story of God revealing himself among people living in community who, despite their proximity, frequently don't get along. Relationships will never come easily, but the wise person realizes our need for them.

Our lives are a web of relationships. We need all kinds of relationships: peer relationships, mentor relationships, mentee relationships. The strongest relationships tend to be with people with whom we've shared an experience or have something in common. It has been my experience that marketplace people need to be in relationship with one another in a unique way. They are enduring the same pressures, passing through the same experiences, and feel alone just as much as anyone else. This chapter should encourage us all to take a look at our relationships and be intentional about the ones we develop.

ED MEESE on
REAGAN AS A MENTOR (bio pp. 259-260)

My most significant mentor was obviously Ronald Reagan. He was more than a person I worked for; he was a mentor from whom I learned a great deal over the thirty years that I worked with him.

Our first meeting came out of the blue. In December 1966, Reagan, having been elected Governor of California, was assembling his staff. I was very happily practicing law in a district attorney's office in Oakland, California. I seemed to be doing well and thought I would spend the rest of my life there. However, somebody remembered my representing all the district attorneys and chiefs of police in California before the state legislature on criminal justice and procedure matters six years earlier. That person recommended me to the incoming governor, and I was asked to meet Reagan and his staff in Sacramento. In the half-hour interview, I was deeply impressed with Governor Reagan—not only his personality, but also the depth of his knowledge about criminal law and criminal justice. We had different ideas about those topics, but our viewpoints meshed. At the end of our meeting, he offered me a job, and I accepted on the spot. I drove home trying to figure out how to explain to my wife that we would be moving to Sacramento. About thirty years later, in September 1997, I visited Reagan for the last time, just before he went into total seclusion due to Alzheimer's disease.

My tenure with Reagan was a tremendous opportunity to learn from a man who also held many positions during his life. He was an Army Reserve Officer and served in World War II. He had been a movie actor, a radio sportscaster, a newspaper columnist, and president of the Screen Actors Guild labor union. He was involved in a variety of political activities, both as a Democrat and as a Republican. He became California's governor, and ultimately, President of the United States. In all of those jobs, he was always concerned about other people, and he was always guided by his religious faith.

People often ask, "What was Ronald Reagan really like?" His tremendous cheerfulness and optimism distinguished him as a leader. I can't remember a time when his optimism didn't surpass the greatest difficulties and even the darkest days that he faced as governor of California or President of the United States. Reagan's cheerfulness was reflected in a tremendous sense of humor. He used jokes and stories to relieve tension, make a point against an opponent, or enliven a speech. It was just part of who he was. If a cabinet meeting got tense and people were at each other's throats, he would often tell a joke so people left the room in a more relaxed frame of mind.

Reagan's optimism did not disregard what was going on around him, the consequences of his decisions, or the tremendous problems that were facing our country. The 1980s were marked by the country's worst economic conditions since the Great Depression. Unemployment was rising beyond 7.5 percent to ten percent, inflation was 12.5 percent, and interest rates were at twenty-one percent. We had a stagnant economy—*stagflation* they called it—something economists previously thought couldn't happen. A tremendous energy shortage was also in full swing. You had to wake up at 5:00 a.m. to line up at a gas station because by 8:30 a.m. the gasoline would be sold out for the day. Those were the conditions that Reagan dealt with, but he was optimistic because of his tremendous faith in God. You don't read much about that because he felt religion was a very private matter. He was not unwilling to discuss it with anybody who raised the topic, but he tried not to raise it deliberately himself because he didn't want people to think he was trying to use his religion for political purposes.

Yet religion was so much a part of Reagan's life that if it came up in conversation, he was able to quote the Bible like very few people I have ever known. He often used religious subjects as illustrations in his speeches. In fact, Reagan made more references to religious or biblical subjects in his speeches than any other U.S. president. In March 1981, as Reagan was recovering from an assassination attempt, he wrote in his diary, "I believe that God has some important things for me to do, and that is why I was spared." From that point forward he had an additional sense of purpose for his life. One of his goals was bringing peace to the conflict with what was then the Soviet Union, a part of history he was primarily responsible for achieving.

DENNIS PEMBERTON on
THE VALUE OF SMALL GROUPS and
MARKETPLACE BIBLE STUDIES (bio p. 263)

The small book club/Bible study I belong to is a great source of spiritual growth. The six men in it are each running their own company or a company's division, raising young families, and dealing with similar issues. Ideally, we would get together weekly, but in reality it's about once every three to four weeks. In the meantime, we call each other. If I have an issue, I can call one of them up and say, "Hey, help me think this through." It's been extremely meaningful to me to know they will approach the problem from a Christian viewpoint. Everyone is in similar phases of life, but going through very different things. One may be going through a divorce, while another's child is very sick. When I think that I've got challenges, I just listen to what other people are going through. That puts things in perspective.

We help one another deal with issues of growing businesses in a world and among people who may not be as ethical or spiritually centered as we are. How do you compete? At what point can you say, "Hold on. Let me take off my Christian hat for a second and deal with this problem. Then I'll put it back on and try to get back in the game"? We try to keep each other on the right path.

I don't know how you can be an entrepreneur and not have faith. Entrepreneurs have to deal with the unknown; they have to reflect on their decisions and the impact it will have on others. How do you survive if you don't believe everything happens for our ultimate good? If you don't believe God guides you, how do you know which way to go when facing tough choices?

ED MEESE on PRAYER BREAKFASTS and SMALL GROUPS (bio pp. 259-260)

It's surprising how many prayer groups there are throughout Washington, DC, including in the U.S. Senate and the House of Representatives. Prayer is one of the few mediating forces at the height of tensions between people of differing political parties and political views. At the weekly Senate and House prayer breakfasts, you will find some of the most virulent partisans on one side of an issue sitting down next to people equally adamant on the other side of the issue. For that hour that they are together, they have a very different attitude towards each other, and to some extent, I believe that spills over into the rest of their day.

You can find many outstanding examples of people in various professions, but particularly in politics, who have been guided by—rather than impeded by—their religious principles. People who also have been willing to take action, sometimes even against the best interests of their so-called political fortunes, on the basis of their religious principles.

I have traveled around the world addressing prayer groups, and I have found that religion means especially a lot to people in the military. The military seems to have a high percentage of people who practice religion. I spent a great deal of time in the military myself, and my son is now a military officer.

In the fall of 1982, a very religious, long-time friend asked if I would be interested in joining a weekly small group for prayer, fellowship, and Bible reading. This was during a very difficult time in my life. My family had recently lost a son in an automobile accident. On top of that, there was significant in-fighting in the White House, and sometimes I became the target of newspaper articles. So I was willing to give the group a try.

My friend told me to be at the Pentagon the next morning at 6:30. I wasn't quite sure what I had signed up for, but I obliged and met my friend and two other men on the Pentagon's steps. We were taken to the office of the Chairman of the Joint Chiefs of Staff, General Jack Vesse. He was the highest-ranking military officer in the United States Armed Forces. When the four of us got together, we mostly talked about our faith and the problems we each faced in our positions. It was a terrific opportunity to get to know each other better.

Up until this point, the Chairman of the Joint Chiefs of Staff and I had sat across the table from one another for several months on the National Security Council, yet I had no idea he was a person of great religious faith. I found we were both Lutherans, and in fact belonged to the same branch of the Lutheran Church. It was a tremendous blessing getting to know him. We have become great friends over the years and worked together on boards of directors of several corporations after he left the Army and I left government.

By 1985, General Vesse had retired from the Army, and I had become Attorney General, so we moved the prayer breakfast to my office. We changed it to 7:00 am Tuesdays and added a few new members. Being in this kind of intimate prayer group offers an experience that I have rarely found any place else. People can say anything and they know it won't be used against them. We make ourselves vulnerable—telling things that we wouldn't tell anybody else in the workplace, maybe things that are even hard to bring up at home—because the other people can relate to what we are going through. In that group, we could talk freely and solve a lot of challenging problems.

For example, one of the most difficult moral issues that I faced was when a former President of the United States wanted to know about a certain political figure who had worked for me. He had been extremely disloyal, had done a bad job, and had some real character defects. The dilemma was: how do you give an honest account to someone who needs to know about this person and yet not have it reflect your personal animosity? How do you do that with a person you have forgiven? We talked that over in our group for about an hour, and they gave me some helpful ideas. I was able to give an honest answer about this person that was consistent with my belief about how a Christian should walk in the love of God.

We decided to expand our group to foreign ambassadors willing to meet to-gether in the name of Jesus. As a result, our Tuesday meetings brought together anywhere from four to ten ambassadors. It has been amazing for me to see the Christian faith that some of them brought with them. And that others, Muslims, Jews, and people who don't ascribe to any particular religious faith were also willing to come together in the name of Jesus. It is probably one of the more ecumenical events that take place in Washington, DC. We are able to talk about international affairs, poverty in certain countries, and so on. We can talk about these things in the spirit of Christ, regardless of people's own particular religious backgrounds. However, we have found that the larger group did not lend itself to the intimacy we found with the smaller group, so six or seven of us also meet an hour before the larger gathering.

I was once at a fairly large prayer meeting with close to twenty attendees in Ja-maica. They told me that half of the people were on one side of the political aisle and half were on the other side. They were mortal enemies in the legislature. The prayer meeting was the one place they could gather in peace and relative harmony.

The three ingredients that all of these small groups have in common are:
1. **Candor**. Nobody is putting up a front or holding anything back. Everyone is honest.
2. **Confidence**. Assurance that what is shared will stay within the group, and people are there to help and support each other.
3. **Comradeship**. The genuine fellowship that you have with people whom you totally trust, whom you totally like, and with whom you can exchange confidences. These people can help you find solutions.

If I could give one piece of advice to all of you who will someday be the magnates of the business world, it is to find a small group of confidants with whom you can have this sort of relationship. It will be beneficial to you throughout your career and throughout your life. The small group does not necessarily need to be com-posed of all men or all women, or only people who are in the same age-range or stage of life. Sometimes it is easier for men, in particular, to talk with other men, and it would be harder for them to share openly about their struggles if women were around, but there is no reason the small groups have to be set up one way or another.

One great experience was in a small group that traveled around Oregon encouraging the formation of these groups among business people. It included three of the most important CEOs in the western part of the United States. One was the owner of a very profitable string of restaurants, another was one of the four co-chairman of the Nordstrom's retail chain, and the third was the president of one of the most important banks in the Midwest. This opportunity to work together with these fine men and to spread the word about small groups was a great opportunity for friendship and living our faith.

KATHERINE FOO on
FELLOWSHIP (bio pp. 254-255)

God has created us to be dependent people—dependent on him and on one another. His proclamation in Genesis that "it is not good for man to be alone" (Genesis 2:18) is a principle that speaks not only to marriage. It pertains to all of life and especially to the spiritual fellowship of all believers. No man or woman is an island. None of us are capable of going about life alone. We need communion with one another.

> *God has arranged the parts in the body, every one of them, just as he wanted them to be. If they were all one part, where would the body be? As it is, there are many parts, but one body.*
> *1 Corinthians 12:18-20*

Also consider this quote from theologian J. I. Packer:

> *We should not . . . think of our fellowship with other Christians as a*
> *spiritual luxury, an optional addition to the exercises of private devotion.*
> *We should recognize rather that such fellowship is a spiritual necessity;*
> *for God has made us in such a way that our fellowship with himself is fed*
> *by our fellowship with fellow-Christians, and requires to be so fed*
> *constantly for its own deepening and enrichment.*

Do we recognize how much we need each other? Do we understand that because of Jesus we share a common life in him? We belong to each other in a relationship. It's important to understand that fellowship is first and foremost a relationship, rather than an activity. The principle is that any activity that follows should come out of that relationship.

> *They were continually devoting themselves to the apostles' teaching*
> *and to fellowship, to the breaking of bread and to prayer.*
> *Acts 2:42 NASB*

The early church was not merely committed to activities, but to relationships. It was through relationship that active sharing was practiced in a myriad of ways. The early Christians didn't just *have* fellowship; they *devoted* themselves to it. To them, fellowship was a clear priority.

Although we may prioritize fellowship with God and with others differently, deep down, all of us recognize our fundamental need for it. And, whether you're a first-year MBA student about to start a summer internship or an established executive, no matter what places you explore, no matter what life experiences you go through, we all need authentic fellowship. We need to discover the joy of sharing ourselves with each other.

ED MEESE on
REINFORCING RELATIONSHIPS (bio pp. 259-260)

The other thing that I want to mention is what I call *reinforcing* relationships. They can be small groups or people with whom you work. In the White House, although we didn't plan it this way, and we didn't have a religious litmus test in hiring, it seems the people who were attracted to these jobs had, for the most part, a strong religious background. You can't always decide who you are going to be working with, but certainly we can encourage colleagues who are of a similar religious faith. It is important in the difficult moments to have people who will support you in creating a workplace atmosphere that is not hostile to people of faith.

Unfortunately, there are workplaces—some of which are encouraged by state laws—that are almost hostile to religion. It is vitally important that people in positions of responsibility make sure this doesn't happen and encourage people in their personal religious faith and practices, as far as such encouragement is within the law and is done without showing favoritism.

Throughout my career people prayed for me, for my family, and for people who were working with me. It is amazing and hugely encouraging when people would recognize me on the street or write to me saying, "I want you to know that I am praying for you." Whenever the newspapers reported on a very tough issue that I was involved in as Attorney General, I would receive a plain envelope with no return address from San Diego, California. Inside would be a piece of lined paper on which was written nothing more than "Psalms 91." That is a powerful Psalm, in which David writes:

> He who dwells in the shelter of the Most High
>   will abide in the shadow of the Almighty.
> I will say to the LORD, "My refuge and my fortress,
>   my God, in whom I trust." . . .

Because you have made the LORD your dwelling place—
the Most High, who is my refuge—
no evil shall be allowed to befall you.

Psalm 91:1-2, 9-10 NKJV

Well, it was kind of comforting just to get that plain piece of paper with Psalms 91, which would remind me again to read that Psalm. It was a tremendous source of support for me.

WENDY MURPHY on
LEARNING THE HARD WAY (bio p. 262)

Early on I really stubbed my toe. I worked in the marketing area of a management-consulting firm, and I was the top producer. I was hitting my stride and was out in front. What I didn't do was spend any time with my colleagues. I felt I was doing the job and doing it well, wasn't that enough?

One Saturday, I came into work and was getting ready for the day. My colleagues didn't come in on Saturdays, and I figured that's why they weren't producing like me. I was very cocky. Just then a database administrator who happened to be passing by leaned over and said, "It's really too bad that you take so many hits. You know, Wendy, they're really trying to do you in." I couldn't believe it. My first reaction was anger, then pain—I was devastated.

Finally, I realized what a real gift it was for that woman to reach out and say that. I became more aware of what was going on. Though I remained a high producer, they did truly want to do me in because my boss decided she didn't like me. Having tried to work it out, I went to the Lord in tears asking for his help. All of a sudden I was offered another job. It was a lateral move to a smaller group. I took it and blossomed. You can be sure I treated my colleagues differently and built lots of relationships. Lesson learned.

what relationships have helped you in life?

join the conversation at www.oursoulsatwork.com/relationships

CHAPTER TEN
PLURALISM

Make it your ambition to lead a quiet life, to mind your own business and to work with your hands, just as we told you, so that your daily life may win the respect of outsiders.

1 Thessalonians 4:11-12a

The United States is a religiously pluralistic society, meaning that all religions are legally allowed. Diversity is an emerging value, and to keep the peace, many businesses have simply sought to eliminate the presence of religion in any way. These environments, devoid of any religious influence, are frequently called *secular*. But *secularism* is distinct from *pluralism*. *Pluralism* is about many faiths; *secularism* is about no faith.

Followers of Christ have often struggled with how to live their faith at work. This struggle is particularly pronounced in workplaces where discussing religion and personal beliefs is discouraged or could even produce hostile reactions. At a young age I learned the axiom, "Never discuss religion or politics in public." Followers of Christ have frequently tended toward two extremes. One extreme is that the workplace is not a place that is particularly relevant to one's faith. The other extreme is that the workplace is something that should somehow be Christianized.

Christian executives and others in positions of leadership have constantly wondered what is appropriate in terms of practicing one's faith at work. Should they seek to turn their company into a Christian company? Should they ever mention their faith? Would being overt about one's faith give the impression that Christ-followers will somehow be favored? But if we don't evangelize, are we compromising our faith?

How to relate to different religions is an under-discussed topic, especially when we consider how central it is to living our faith in a meaningful way at work. In this chapter some of the concepts may be challenging, but I hope the end result is that we will not ignore the issue of faith at work, but will have a more robust understanding for how we can live faithfully in a diverse and complex world.

JEFF RUSSELL on CREATING
A PLURALISTIC BUSINESS CULTURE (bio pp. 264-265)

Easy Office is a social venture providing affordable finance, accounting, and bookkeeping services to nonprofits nationwide. We are a business service provider, i.e., an outsourcing company that sells people's time and expertise. We have no research and development department, no real fixed assets, no patents, no unique technology. As a people business, human resource (HR) strategy is front and center as the most important aspect of our success. Our business is based on identifying a neglected market niche, building a business model to support that market niche, and creating the operational platform and team to deliver to that niche. Creating the team to do that is my most important job as CEO.

I have grown up and lived by the Christian faith tradition all of my life. Being raised in the Deep South Bible Belt, growing up in this tradition comes as no surprise. Since leaving the South and traveling the world, I have continued to strive to live out my faith daily. After I graduated from college, I wrestled with whether I should be a missionary to the tribes of Papua New Guinea or if I should be a businessperson. I thought it was an either/or decision. Through a series of events, I came to realize that this choice did not have to be made; I could do and be both. I worked in the business world for ten years accumulating experience as a consultant, and then ran the Asian division of a multi-national company in Bangkok.

While in Bangkok, I looked out the windows of my twenty-seventh-floor, air-conditioned office onto a four-square-mile slum community home to nearly a million people. During the day, I worked tirelessly to make sure shoeboxes showed up on time, the cost of leather for our clients was as low as possible, and the packaging wouldn't fall apart during transit. But in the quiet still moments, I would stare out of my window looking down at the slum community, wondering what difference I had made. Some kid in Des Moines had some sweet, inexpensive, athletic shoes. So what? The fire burned within me to be more directly involved in something social.

After Bangkok, I spent two years pursuing my MBA at Yale. The Yale School of Management tag line is "Leaders for Business and Society," so it was a perfect fit for me. I came in with the idea for Easy Office and took copious notes in every class, relating each lesson to what Easy Office should be. During this time, more than twenty people—about ten percent of my class—donated time to improving our business plan. As we developed that plan and reflected on its potential over the course of those two years, it became clear to me that our HR strategy was essential. I wanted to be very intentional regarding the culture we built. As a start-up, we had the unique opportunity to build something from the inside out.

The volunteer Yale team came from predictably diverse religious backgrounds. Our ranks included Hindus, Buddhists, agnostics, atheists, Christians, and Jews. I knew I wanted Easy Office to reflect this diversity on an on-going basis. Although my Christian faith is important to me, I know it is individuals who must embrace faith for it to be meaningful, not the institution they work for. A person is a Buddhist or a Christian; an organization is neither. It is possibly made up of people of a single religion, but the organization reflects the people, not the other way around. My goal was to build a company that was truly pluralistic, not secular. I wanted religion and faith to be something that was openly discussed, not something that was hidden under the table.

As a social venture working exclusively with nonprofits, we recognized that our clients' values often conflict with each other, and may conflict with our own personal values. We chose to embrace this reality, not fight against it. In every interview I conduct for Easy Office, I tell the following story:

> One of the unique aspects of Easy Office is that our clients may have views that conflict with each other, or conflict with your own. For example, I was in Bozeman, Montana, a few years ago, meeting with the Predators Conservation Alliance. They wanted to save the wolves. The next day I met with the Cattleman Ranchers' Association, and they wanted to shoot every wolf in sight. I'd love to have both as clients. I'm from Mississippi, and my grandfather had cattle, but there are no wolves

there, so it is not an emotional issue for me even though it is a highly charged issue for some people.

At this point the interviewee typically laughs and says something like, "Yes, I'm a very open person and know that not everyone agrees with me." One interviewee—that I hired, by the way—told me that she worked for the Cattleman Association, and her family gets authorization from the government to hunt wolves from helicopters. She told me that she was willing to work with Predators Conservation Alliance, but that she wouldn't be donating any money to them!

The interview continues:

> To take it a step further, maybe wolves are not an issue you get emotional about, but when you get into religion and politics, people can be more sensitive. I come from a Christian faith tradition; Amy, my partner, is Jewish. Folks in the company come from all different backgrounds. We also serve clients of varying religions. One is a missionary in Asia, and we put Bible verses on her donation receipts. We serve multiple Jewish nonprofits along with a nonprofit in New York City focused on advancing Muslim causes. We've sent proposals to the Society to Abolish the Death Penalty, and we've sent proposals to Prevention Works, a needle-exchange program. We have clients who seek to evangelize Mexico, and some that seek to provide more alternatives for people with alternative sexual orientation. Easy Office is a place where "cause" and "beliefs" are all out in the open. Because of our clients, we could have it no other way.

At this point, some interviewees squirm. Those we don't hire. Some have told me that they won't work for atheists or groups that promote controversial causes. Those we don't hire. But most people smile and acknowledge that they enjoy working with groups of differing views; they understand that working for nonprofits is different than working with restaurants or other small businesses, and most people express surprise and appreciation regarding our openness.

Any HR strategy is more than just "selection." It is also about retention, rewards and recognition, recruitment, training, and performance management. Dr. Jim Baron, Yale professor and HR guru, constantly beat us over the head that HR strategies must be tailored to each unique business strategy; they must be in sync with the business culture of each company. If longevity with clients is important, don't hire contractors to interact with your clients. If clients are extremely price sensitive, as nonprofits are, don't build an HR strategy around paying the highest wages in town.

We have worked hard to make sure our entire HR system stays in sync with those we serve. For example, we don't provide employees with Christmas Eve and Christmas day off. Those are certainly considered American holidays, but are also uniquely Christian. What do our Jewish employees really care about Christmas and the birth of Jesus? So to be consistent, we allow three flex days from September to December that can be used for Christmas, Hanukkah, or to go skiing.

We pay below market wages, but try to make up for it with flexibility and other benefits such as providing a week of paid time off for people to volunteer at a nonprofit of their choice. People who don't value volunteering aren't going to value this benefit, are going to feel under-rewarded, and are going to self-select *out of* working for Easy Office. People who do value this benefit, will enjoy this perk, feel appropriately rewarded, and will self-select *into* working for Easy Office. These are exactly the type of people we want to attract.

The HR strategy of any social venture needs to be carefully considered. If it is a "business as mission" company that serves an expressly religious purpose, the HR strategy may be different than our own. We exist to help all nonprofits—regardless of cause or creed—become more effective and efficient.

If and when we come across nonprofits that I personally feel are violating some of Jesus' teaching, and they want Easy Office's help, we still help. We do so because I am personally convinced that we should be salt in the world, not excluding ourselves or hiding from the world. Jesus' example shows interaction with all types of folks from all walks of life and belief systems. My goal is to mold Easy Office to mirror this same spirit of love and inclusiveness. In doing so, I personally believe we are helping live out the words of Jesus in helping others to clothe the naked, feed the hungry, house the homeless, and to help the prisoners, widows, and orphans.

MATTHEW McCREIGHT on THRIVING AS A CHRISTIAN IN A SECULAR COMPANY (bio p. 259)

Being a Christian in management consulting, particularly in a secular company, is something I think about and work on purposefully.

First, it helps to be in a place that values you for who you are, not for what you might be. How can you tell? Look at the partners who run the company. If they are not leading the life that you want to lead, then you're going to have a very tough time leading the kind of life you value. You might be able to change them, but it will be slow and difficult. You might work in such a place for a few years to gain experience, but be careful. It's easy for a few years to become ten, and you discover you are the one who has changed.

I came to Robert H. Shaffer & Associates, LLC for that very reason. I looked at the senior people in the firm. Some of the senior people actually had outside lives. One is a devout Jew and very successful. That said to me it may be a challenging place, but it values me. Other people with similar values have been successful. The firm has been supportive of my faith.

Second, as a Christian in a place where you're involved in lots of important things, and perhaps even own your firm, the choices you make bear intense scrutiny. People know I'm a Christian and that my wife is a priest. When I do things, I know I am representing the faith, even if passively. At the very least, I don't want to do harm, and at best, I want people to be encouraged that my faith is something worth considering. My faith influences how I approach my work all of the time.

Having said all of that, there are real challenges. How do you fire someone in a "Christian" way? It's tough. That's why prayer, thought, community, and grounding are important to draw on when things get intense. The instincts of the world are usually going to be different than the instincts of a Christian.

Third, being in business provides tremendous opportunity to help your church, whether it's teaching, serving, or giving. Give generously to the places around you. With a busy job, trying to support my wife in all her work and life, and our kids in theirs, and being involved in our local church, I have to choose outside activities pretty carefully so I don't end up shortchanging everyone—especially my family!

One place I invest my time is on the board of the Overseas Ministry Study Center, based in New Haven. It's a marvelous place where church leaders from around the world come to Yale for a semester of rest, further study, and renewal. The things you see going on in the Christian world are amazing. Seeing how other people are living out their lives challenges your assumptions about what it means to build your faith. I would encourage you to get involved and to learn from other people in other cultures, particularly as the center of Christianity shifts toward Asia and Africa.

Years ago, my wife gave me *A Traveler's Prayer Book* to keep me company on my many trips. This is an excerpt from something written by the English priest and poet, John Donne, in the early 1600s:

> *The blessedness of having studied and learned and practiced the knowledge of God's purpose shall endure forever. When you shall turn from the left to the right side on your death bed, from all the honors and riches of this world to breathe your soul into those hands that gave it,*

this righteousness, this good conscience shall endure then and meet you in the gate of heaven. Accustom yourself to find the presence of God in all your getting, in all your preferments, in all your studies, and God will be abundantly sufficient for you in all.

DAVID MILLER on CHAPLAINS
IN THE WORKPLACE (ESPECIALLY TYSON) (bio pp. 260-261)

I've been doing research for a book I'm writing on the growing phenomenon of workplace chaplains. There are hospital chaplains and military chaplains, but believe it or not, there has been a surge of interest in recent years in workplace chaplains. John Tyson's program at Tyson Foods is distinct because John manages it in house, whereas most companies hire a third party chaplaincy agency. Most of the third party agencies only offer Christian chaplains, but will refer you to a chaplain of another tradition if your employees request it. But John actually has had a Muslim Imam as one of his chaplains because one plant had a majority Muslim population, which stays true to being faith-friendly. It's extraordinary. Some of these plant managers are burly, tough, no nonsense, rough guys who have no time for the touchy-feely stuff. Initially, some didn't like the idea of workplace chaplains. They soon changed their minds. And now during a period of economic retrenchments and budget cuts, they're saying, "You take away my chaplain over my dead body!" Even on razor fine margins they want to keep their chaplains.

DAVID MILLER on
CREATING FAITH-FRIENDLY BUSINESSES (bio pp. 260-261)

Bill Pollard, who is the retired chairman and CEO of the ServiceMaster Company, used to do devotions before he opened board meetings. He and I co-founded and launched The Avodah Institute that brings together CEOs and senior executives in small settings to talk about a single question: "How do we integrate the claims of our faith with the demands of our work?" In one of the sessions, our theme was "Making Your Company Faith-Friendly." I asked, "What might this really look like in a world of publicly traded companies?"

Some view this idea of making a company faith-friendly problematic. Yet my research has revealed that embracing new and at-first controversial ideas is not new to leading businesses. Back in the 1960s, enlightened, smart companies came to terms with racism. Racism was institutionalized and legal in this country, but the smart companies embraced integration and became race-friendly. In the 1970s, the big issue was women. The *Equal Rights Amendment* failed to pass, but progressive companies tried to get rid of their prejudices and become female-friendly. The 1980s was the decade of being family-friendly, where companies created daycare centers and flex time so employees didn't have to come into the office if their kids were sick in the morning, or stay at work when their kids' soccer games were going on. They developed family-friendly policies so employees' careers wouldn't be harmed even if they had additional family responsibilities because they were divorced. Companies began to realize that the whole employee mattered, that their entire well-being determined how well they would perform at work. They wanted to welcome the whole employee into the workplace.

The 1990s saw the arrival of the gay, lesbian, bisexual, and transgender community. Thirty years ago it would have been career suicide to talk about one's same-sex orientation. Regardless what you think theologically about the subject of "gay lifestyles," these people exist—whether publicly declared or not—in every workplace. Companies had to decide whether to ignore that sexual orientation issues were a reality, or address them by considering fair and equitable policies and practices. To divide your employees into two groups that you care for differently is a theologically problematic concept, regardless of where you stand on the gay question.

Today, all of these workplace taboos—race, gender, family demands, and gender orientation—have been broken. Things that you would never before dream of talking about are now being addressed. Enlightened companies want the whole person to come to work. In my work with companies like Deloitte, PepsiCo, and Tyson Foods, I have been pressing this question: If you really believe in diversity, inclusion, and all the related words in your literature, you've got to come to terms with how you embrace the spiritual side of being human. From the most ancient philosophers to the greatest thinkers, successful civilizations have been built on the understanding that people are comprised of mind, body, and spirit. To pretend that people don't have a spiritual dimension is false. So how do we think about it? What do we do with it? How does spirituality and worldviews fit into the diversity and inclusion movement?

It is possible—and practical—for companies to be faith-friendly by acknowledging people's spiritual side and setting up policies and practices that legitimize—but don't give special privilege to—people of various religious traditions. It's similar to how companies legitimized racial minorities, working mothers, divorced parents, and gays in the workplace.

JOHN TYSON on
FAITH-FRIENDLY WORKPLACE (bio pp. 267-268)

We experienced an interesting situation shortly after we first communicated our Core Values to our employees. The Tyson helpline got a call, "I'm an atheist, and you don't leave any room for the Muslims, Buddhists, Jews, etc." The caller's list included everything but Christians. It was a fair observation. As we prepared to respond, it became very clear to us that the purpose of a faith-friendly environment, one of our Core Values, is to allow *all* faiths to participate in the workplace.

Within our company of 107,000 folks, we have a variety of faith traditions, including Muslim, Jewish, atheist, and agnostic populations, but most of our team members are Christian, due to the location of our plants (across the South and the Midwest). Striving to be faith-friendly provides respect and room for all of these populations. Now, we have operations in Mexico, China, Brazil, and India, as well as Europe. As we strive to be a faith-friendly company and honor God, we're trying to create an environment where it is acceptable to live your faith in the workplace. Our hope is that different faiths will enter true dialogue instead of polarizing discussions.

The reason our chaplaincy program has grown at Tyson Foods is that it's a program of attraction. It's not required. It's not mandated. When we first started out, we only had five or six chaplains. Now, we have about 150 chaplains and other faith leaders covering sixty to seventy percent of our locations. We've had to go through some adjustments in our company because the marketplace has been a little tough, but one of the things company managers have chosen not to cut has been our chaplaincy program. It has taken on its own life and is an important part of who we are and how we live. That's a testament to what we can do as business leaders by trying to create an environment of permission for all faiths to coexist in the workplace.

We've worked purposefully to avoid establishing an affinity for one group over another. We are a faith-friendly organization that gives permission for all faiths, not just Christian or Islamic groups. It is an integrated deal—holistic to our organization versus an affinity for one group that puts people in a box. There's a tendency to create programs that isolate groups instead of a faith-friendly culture that integrates. You have to fight through that.

Our chaplains and leaders of other faiths are part-time with us and full-time within their own religious groups. One of the questions I ask all the chaplains is, "Why do you want to be a chaplain at Tyson Foods? Why would you want to do this, since you already have a full-time job at the church?" Most tell me the chaplaincy work allows them to get back to the front lines and carry their ministry into the workplace. It gets them out of being in the church building all of the time—i.e., checking the books in the pews and all the other duties that go along with being a minister of a church—and back to what they always thought they were going to do, which was to help people try to move forward in their day-to-day lives. Maybe Bill and Mary are having difficulties because Bill drinks too much or Mary is not being faithful, or their son's having a challenge with addictive issues. Our chaplains are there to help them walk through whatever they are facing five days a week instead of just one. We didn't have a great game plan to begin with, but this is the way the chaplaincy has evolved.

People ask how we justify the cost of a workplace chaplaincy. Our plants, which usually consist of between five hundred and one thousand team members, are very aware of cost and margins. If we make two to four percent profit, it's a good year. The fact that the chaplaincy has gone from six chaplains to one hundred fifty through voluntary participation by plant managers is a tremendous indicator of its value. The program allows for early intervention in conflict. Our HR folks are involved with insurance, claims, and team member guidelines. The chaplains give team members a confidential ear and have the time to sit and listen. We have not had a single manager opt out of the plan to save money.

There's now enough measured evidence to demonstrate the plants are healthier because we have these ministers around to take on some tough issues. Our workforce is semi-skilled to unskilled. We have eighteen different languages spoken in our plants as well as a lot of political refugees, people from Sudan, Somalia, and Central America, just to name a few. We are a micro-picture of what America looks like.

A few years ago, over in Sudan a helicopter got shot down while carrying a leader of a Sudanese tribe. Before we knew it, that issue came to the floor in a beef plant, which had a significant Sudanese employee base. One tribe thought the other tribe had shot down their leader. We weren't prepared for it, but because we had chaplains on the plant floor, we were able to enter the debate and have some cultural and religious familiarity with how to handle the issue. Another interesting dynamic is Sudanese men will not take orders from women, and we have a lot of women leaders in our plants doing quality assurance and supervising. The chaplains often help bridge these issues by encouraging dialogue.

Faith in the workplace can work anywhere. Here are some basic principles that have helped us: First, avoid getting pigeonholed as an "affinity" program. Second, try to create an environment in which all faiths are permissible, whatever they may be. Third, it takes core people, not only at the senior level, but in middle to lower-level management. They're the ones to take ownership.

When we started this program, I had many discussions about whether I should mandate the chaplaincy program, but my personal experience led me to let the program sell itself without forcing the issue. We let the managers start talking to each other. When they started to share what they saw, we heard anecdotal examples of how the atmosphere had changed on the plant floor, stories of people working together. That's how we've gotten to where we are. If it comes from the top down, people feel like you're pushing religion on them, and they don't buy in. When we gave it our support and just laid it out there, it started to build momentum and has carried itself without our giving it any more emphasis.

DENNIS PEMBERTON on
BUILDING A FAITH-FRIENDLY ENVIRONMENT (bio p. 263)

We are an investment advisory firm focusing on alternative investment. Currently, the investments are primarily real estate and hedge funds. The firm has grown into a place that I really value. I've always wanted it to be a fun place where people feel comfortable and loved.

Growing up, our community was very diverse. We had large Jewish and international populations, plus many residents who worked in the United Nations. This exposed me to a variety of religions and cultures from a young age. My passion for creating an environment where people can be free to worship and feel their culture is respected was born in those early years.

In my firm, I am open about being a Christian, but our firm is very faith-friendly, regardless of what kind it is. I am extremely fascinated by learning about other religions and encourage people to share their experiences, their traditions, cultures, and holidays. What they bring is very valuable to me. As CEO and a Christian, I set the tone. I try to lead by example by creating a work environment that is very open—and that works for us.

STEVE REINEMUND on
DIVERSITY IN THE WORKPLACE (bio p. 264)

A few years ago, I gave a half-hour talk about the importance of diversity in business to an audience of five hundred students at Stanford University. During the question-and-answer session, the first student said, "I am convinced that you believe diversity is good for business. My question is: Would you do it if it weren't good for business?"

I answered that diversity is important in business. However, the student stood up again and said, "You didn't answer my question." So I went back and tried to answer his question again. The next student stood up and said, "In all due respect, you still didn't answer that question." Despite that rough start we went on and had a great discussion, but it continued to bother me long after the session concluded that I hadn't been able to find the words to really express what I thought on that subject.

Several of my colleagues serve as sounding boards for me on different issues. I discussed the incident with them, but none of them were able to fully explain why I felt so uncomfortable expressing my dedication to diversity whether it was good for business or not. Then one day, while I was on my treadmill—which is where I do my best thinking—it became clear. I had only addressed the business side—the head side—of the issue. I forgot that most issues of any importance have both a head side and a heart side. Hopefully, the students realized I believed in supporting diversity whether it was good or bad for business, although I was unable to state that clearly. I had felt I was supposed to focus only on the business side, or the head side, so I was unable to adequately address the student's question because I wasn't answering from my heart.

Yes, diversity is good for business. There is no question about that, and my belief in that fact is rooted in my personal life story. Although I grew up with no money, I didn't realize I was poor. My family had very little, and it was tough at times, but I began to recognize that I had a chance at a better life when certain people began leveling the playing field for me and giving me a fair chance to compete with those around me. At those times, I knew my economic status did not need to determine my future.

When I ran for student council, for instance, all the other candidates were wearing sports coats as they gave their speeches, but I wasn't. So a teacher gave me his coat and leveled the playing field. Such opportunities planted the seeds for my commitment to diversity and memories like that still make me emotionally committed to diversity today.

For better or worse, our life stories—what we really believe and what is fundamental to who we are—become evident when we are leaders. As leaders in business and society, we have an opportunity to incorporate our moral and ethical values into the work we do. We have to find our own way while also setting an example for our employees. Being a CEO has allowed me to combine my personal ambitions, thoughts, and values with what was ultimately best for the business. It is a responsibility I can never take lightly.

what are your thoughts on
religious pluralism?

join the conversation at
www.oursoulsatwork.com/pluralism

CHAPTER ELEVEN
ETHICS

"Honesty lives confident and carefree, but Shifty is sure to be exposed. "

Proverbs 10:9 THE MESSAGE

Some things are morally black and white, but the vast majority of our lives exist in a grey area of ethical ambiguity. When looking at ethically challenging situations, I have noticed that people removed from the situation tend to lean toward being more absolute—i.e., more black and white on what is right or wrong—whereas people in the situation lean toward being more relativistic—i.e., it's grey, so not knowing exactly what they should do, they are more open to doing anything.

It is tempting to look at certain situations and simply say that there is no way to know, so do as you wish—or to go to the other extreme and always hold a hard line. Neither is particularly productive, however, if the goal is to be a sincere follower of Christ.

Every issue has at least two sides that should be considered. Is it okay to produce food products which are not healthy? Who defines healthy? Where are the lines we should draw? Are there ethical guidelines that Christ followers should adhere to for processing animals? Is there a standard framework through which we should make our decisions?

A chapter on ethics should never attempt to completely eliminate the tension. The tension will always be there due to the complexities of life. Nor should it be communicated that there is a single solution to every problem. Nevertheless, when we do not think these issues through, our chances of doing what is right, holy, and just is seriously diminished.

WENDY MURPHY on
CEO ETHICS AND THE CEO'S CONSCIENCE (bio p. 262)

The Chief Human Resources Officer's role has changed largely because of the *Sarbanes-Oxley Act* (which was passed in 2002 to increase corporate responsibility and transparency in the light of the scandals at such companies as Enron, Tyco International, Adelphia, Peregrine Systems, and WorldCom), executive compensation debates, succession planning, and talent issues. The most important person the CEO has on his right or left side is now the Chief HR Officer. This officer virtually acts as the CEO's conscience, and along with the CFO, helps guide the CEO's decisions, strategies, and policies. It's a new triumvirate: CEO, CFO, and Chief HR Officer. Aligning those people and finding a good HR person who will be that filter is a huge responsibility. That is the task of my job: I find the right HR people for the firms that hire us.

When I'm doing such a search, I spend a lot of time with the CEO and sometimes with the board of directors trying to understand what's important to the organization and what their values are. I take what I learn from these interactions with me to the interview process. With ten candidates on a slate at any given time, the challenge is to discover what really makes them tick. That's often very hard to determine with Chief HR Officers, because they are skilled interviewers and are often "people-people." They know how to give the answers I am looking for as opposed to what they might actually think. Yet some of the best Chief HR Officers are not necessarily people-people. They are business leaders who understand the alignment of people and strategy, and how to leverage human capital towards an end goal.

HR Officers have to be willing to answer questions like: How would you go about laying people off? What decisions are being made around the CEO and how would you be part of them? Would you turn a blind eye to something you should be confronting people about? Would you ignore what's going on with the behavior of the CEO or with the senior leadership team in order to stay in favor with them?

Chief HR officers are much more than they used to be. In essence, it is now up to them to be the keeper of the brand and conscience of the culture in their organizations, even though you would never think of that being in their job description. It's a huge responsibility. However, too often they do sell out, cover up, and sweep things under the rug in order to protect their positions or their relationships with upper management. They don't look at the ethical issues for the same reasons other chief officers don't, and in today's marketplace that can only eventually lead to disaster.

I pray about these things. I have had to rescind offers to prospective candidates—in fact three in the past month and a half—for poor referencing and poor compensation information. That's a lot of rescinding, which means there's a lot of dishonesty or inaccurate references being given to me, perhaps with the thought I will never really check to verify the information. However, I do a lot of referencing, and I believe that God through the Holy Spirit gives me guidance in everything I do and helps me truly see into the character of each person I interview. It's important to find and place HR executives who will serve the CEO and company with integrity. Companies depend on this now more than ever before.

WENDY MURPHY on
CEO COMPENSATION (bio p. 262)

CEO compensation is a constant dilemma because the question is more, "What are you worth in the marketplace?" than "What do you think is fair?" When you talk about compensating executives, CEOs will always say, "I want them to understand what market pricing is." That's a tough one. It is always a balance between what executives can command in a competitive marketplace, what's fair, and what's honorable.

A lot of salaries and overall compensation packages are off the wall, but in a capitalist society, the most qualified candidates have to be well rewarded in order to attract them to any particular company. Part of me says, "More power to them," and the other part says, "This screams of greed." It's a dilemma. We spend hours talking about it. Committees in our company constantly brief us on what the market really looks like. Once packages have already gone up and up and up, what do you do? Too often you are forced to do what the market dictates or else lose a candidate you really want. It's a tough issue.

JOHN TYSON on
ANIMAL RIGHTS (bio pp. 267-268)

To organize an agricultural system and put quality food products on the table is an honor that God has given Tyson Foods. The simple fact is we have to kill animals as a part of that process. How to humanely handle the animals is an ongoing challenge. We are gaining knowledge in this area every day.

One debate is over the use of electrical stunning versus controlled atmospheric stunning in order to lessen the pain caused to our animals. Scientists say electrical stunning is okay, but another group says you should use controlled atmosphere. However, there are technical and quality issues with controlled atmosphere stunning. With electrical stunning, the body continues to pump the blood out of the system to help clean it in preparation for being packaged. With controlled atmosphere stunning, however, the muscles stop working so you immediately start to lose the quality of the product because the blood stays in the muscles after the animal dies. When you get into what the animal actually feels in the process, there have been no scientific studies that say one method is significantly different from the other.

There are also considerable debates on the humane way to raise animals in an industry like ours. We work with only three meat-producing animals: hogs, cattle, and poultry. As far as vertical integration, our focus is poultry. The issue of proper spacing—free range versus confinement spacing—is more complicated than one might think. For example, consider the so-called bird flu issue, which was a problem primarily in Malaysia, Indonesia, and China. In those regions, it was transmitted for the most part from human to human in populations living with their animals. Various international trade and scientific organizations believe the best solution would be to move to the Western style of raising animals: contained farms. However, this would change the entire social structure in those communities because they have been living this way for generations. When somebody has one hundred chickens, they can go to the marketplace and exchange their product for a bag of rice and a couple of T-shirts. Western-style farming would take that away. It gets very complicated when we also start to talk about animal health issues, trade-offs, and the expectations people have about their food.

Nevertheless, Tyson Foods is committed to the well-being, proper handling, and humane slaughter of all the animals that are used in our food products. This is a long-standing commitment, and we pledge our diligence in leading the industry pursuit of new and improved technologies and methods to further enhance animal well-being. This is not only the right thing to do, but is an important moral and ethical obligation we owe to our suppliers, to our customers, to ourselves, and most of all to the animals we depend on for our products and our livelihood. All Tyson team members, as well as our poultry growers and beef and pork suppliers, are expected to respect and steward the animals we work with every day, treating them in a proper manner at all times.

STEVE REINEMUND on
OBESITY (bio p. 264)

In order to live we all have to eat and drink. As CEO and Chairman at PepsiCo, I was steeped in the food and beverage industry. I spent a lot of time with nutritionists. We acknowledged obesity as an issue from the very beginning. In terms of health and wellness in developed countries and increasingly in under-developed countries, it is probably the most important, preventable, long-term health and wellness issue.

We wanted to be a part of the solution. However, the most realistic nutritionists recognize that no one consumes food as if they were a robot. The nutritionists who have the best success in helping people live balanced lives are the ones that help people understand how to make wise food and beverage choices. We wanted to be part of that.

Of particular importance is the challenge of finding a solution for kids. When I was in school, we were never taught proper nutrition. Most of our parents understood it instinctively and provided proper meals, but it wasn't nearly as scientific as you would expect in a civilization as developed as ours. We presented proper nutrition guidelines, particularly in schools, and especially in inner-city schools where the biggest problems exist. Statistics show that obesity is severe in general, but it is most severe in minority and inner-city communities.

At the same time, we reviewed our whole portfolio, whether we commercially benefit from making those changes or not. For example, we took trans fats out of all of the Frito Lay products as a result of our own research before consumers even knew what trans fats were. We didn't advertise the change because nobody knew what it was. I remember explaining to the board of directors that I was going to spend $50 million to take the trans fats out of Frito Lay. I wasn't sure I was going to survive the day—they thought I was nuts. Nobody knew what trans fats were, but our scientific board did research that showed trans fats were a growing issue and part of the growing obesity problem in the United States, so we eliminated trans fats from our product line.

We also created a classification for our products to help consumers make better food choices. A little green spot on PepsiCo products signifies they are healthier products based on standards set by the National Academy of Science. That spot is on forty-two percent of our products sold in the United States.

Originally we took the idea of standards to the Grocery Manufacturers Association, but I quickly realized my life isn't going to be long enough to get standards established through that channel, so we just did it ourselves. Eventually, the industry will come together on a simple set of standards, but it will take some time.

We also developed truly nutritional, value-added types of products. We bought companies with those capabilities like Stacey's Pita Chips in Boston and Naked Juice. Over time, we want to have a portfolio that has true balance to it. In the U.S., we are pretty balanced; but in some of the other countries, we are still only moving towards balance.

We believe that we have a choice. We believe in transparency. We believe in education. And we believe that as a responsible company, we can be part of the solution and not the problem, so we started taking steps towards that before anyone else even started thinking we should.

JEFF METZNER on
AN ETHICAL FRAMEWORK (bio p. 260)

A complete ethical view comprises three major ethical schools of thought. It must be:

1. principle-based,
2. concerned about both the means as well as the ends, and
3. malleable to situational dynamics, addressing the right, the good, and the appropriate.

At different times in my life I have favored each school of thought. For most of my childhood, my religious exposure was limited to the Catholic tradition. I became involved more broadly in Christianity as a young adult, but I continued to judge most ethical dilemmas as black and white cases of right or wrong. University studies pushed me from this black and white perspective to a larger focus on considering the means as well as the end. A philosophy major led me to appreciate Aristotle's notion that the pursuit of virtue is an end in itself.

My conception of ethics has two main aspects:

1. ethics involves a concern for both process and outcome, and
2. ethics is fundamentally about a series of actions, not about a theory or a single moment-in-time decision.

On the first point, I am reminded how a crowd of people described Jesus: "He has done all things well" (Mark 7:37, NASB). They said this in response to the excellence and breadth of Jesus' ministry. This idea of the pursuit of excellence is core to how I view ethics.

It has been said that we are known by those around us for who we are rather than what we would like others to think about us. Thus the study of ethics is the framework used to guide all of my actions, but it is also informed by and shaped by the actions themselves, as my actions define a meaningful part of who I am.

What is the source of my ethics?

My ethics are founded on the Christian faith tradition. I was raised in a family steeped in the Catholic tradition and have turned to nondenominational Christian churches in my adulthood for guidance and encouragement in matters of faith. Since the Bible is my guiding text, some of the most basic biblical stories are foundational to how I approach ethics.

For example, I believe that man and woman are created by an omniscient, omnipresent God who is also involved in their everyday life. This means that the Creator did not set life in motion, sit back, and watch things start to unwind. He is interested in the minutiae of life and desires that his creation will seek to live life abundantly. (See John 10:10.)

God's continued involvement with creation is important for my ethical worldview. For instance, it leads me to the conclusion that God is interested in the ethical dilemmas I face. I can therefore use prayer and teachings from biblical texts as resources when I come against tough decisions in the workplace.

Two important biblical teachings that help form my ethics are the existence of evil and the possibility of redemption. The Christian tradition holds that humankind is inherently flawed, separate from God in our natural state, and prone to acts of evil. One implication of the existence of evil is that I can expect to frequently face situations in business which are the result of unethical behavior in both others and myself. Another implication of the presence of evil is that I can expect there will be people I come across in business who want to intentionally harm my family and/or me.

This is not a fatalistic view, but rather an acknowledgement that I will be tempted in situations to reply to an unethical affront with an unethical response of my own. I need to decide before I am in that situation what I will do, because once I am in an ethical pinch, it may already be too late.

We all know the story of the frog in boiling water. I take to heart the admonishment that the more I have decided beforehand about where the water starts to turn warm on my ethical scale, the better prepared I will be to do the right thing if the time ever comes.

The Bible describes the story of redemption in great length, whereby we have an opportunity to be reconciled to God as a result of his own mercy. This also influences my thinking on ethics. Since I have received a second chance—and third, and fourth, *ad infinitum*—to be reconciled with the Creator's cosmic order, I want to allow room for letting grace take precedence at times over a hard-fact pattern that would favor judgment over mercy.

The Christian beliefs in the inherent worth of mankind, our fallen natural state, and our opportunities for redemption are all foundational to my faith and my way of ethical reasoning. They form a deep bedrock for my ethics and encourage me to treat each individual with fundamental respect, to be on guard against unethical tendencies in both myself and others, and lead me to take a big-picture view of those caught in ethical wrong doing.

What is my ethical framework?

The first part of an ethical framework must deal with where to set the ethical alarm bells. I need to know when to proceed with caution, and I need to know long before it is too late. In the business world, we frequently hear about following the *The Wall Street Journal* test: "Do not act in a way you would not like to read about on the front page of the *The Wall Street Journal*."

Sherron Watkins' "3Ms" test is more rigorous: "Do not act in a way you would not want to tell your *mother*, your *mentor*, or the *media* about." Given the source of my ethics, though, my personal test needs to be more aligned with what David Eisner, CEO of TheMarkets.com, recently said, "To make holy the name of the Lord in the world." *Will my action bring honor to God—or will it bring shame?*

If the answer is not immediately clear, my next step is to look in depth at the situation through an ethical framework. Edwin Epstein describes it well with this phrase, "Does it acknowledge the dignity—better still, the *divinity*—of each individual?" This statement is not about elevating humans to divine stature; rather, it's recognizing that if we each have received life because of God, we are all worthy of fundamental respect regardless of circumstances.

For his part, God has said, "You shall be holy for I the Lord your God am holy" (Leviticus 19:2, NKJV). We should be in the pursuit of excellence in both process and result. If I genuinely hold my actions to this measure, I will often fall short, but this is the standard of ethical conduct that aligns most completely with my faith.

The principles guiding my ethical framework, then, are:

1. a deep and uncompromising respect for all persons,
2. a belief in the value of multiple opinions on ethical matters, and
3. the belief that God's holiness is the standard for all my conduct.

The final aspect of my ethical framework is that any ethical dilemma should serve to inform future decisions. While part of this can be captured in storytelling, I believe that once the dust has cleared from any situation, the decision makers should discuss lessons learned from both the process and the outcome of how they responded to that situation. Only when we are willing to learn from the past can we hope to reach the standard of excellence to which we are called.

What is my public language for ethics?

There are three parts to my public language for ethics:

1. my standard of conduct,
2. the values behind that standard, and
3. the source of those values.

First, the most important part of my ethical framework is the holiness command from Leviticus. While "be holy for I am holy" probably will not resonate much with those of other faith backgrounds, interpreting that verse along the lines of excellence does resonate with virtually everyone. *Excellence* is a concept employers fully support and usually encourage in their own description of their company's values, principles, and guidelines. Excellence is also easy to discuss with co-workers. It is a concept that is understood and respected. Virtually anyone who knows of Tiger Woods, regardless of their affinity for golf, respects Tiger because he executes each of his golf shots with unparalleled excellence. Excellence is also something that I am comfortable relating closely to my faith.

At times, I may need to discuss more than a vague notion of excellence and I believe the clarifying level is a discussion of values. Here I can discuss respect for individuals and grace—in other words, appropriately allowing for opportunities of redemption in the workplace for those who have made mistakes or misjudgments. These and other values, such as the dichotomy between good and evil, are widely held and can be spoken about in a manner that is not specifically reverential to one faith tradition over that of another.

There may be times when I need or choose to go even deeper as I speak about my ethics, when I need to address the source of my values. In some situations, I first need to address what does not motivate my adherence to certain values. My motivation for living ethically should not be because I think it will help me to succeed financially, but rather it should be about doing the right thing. The problem with saying that "the good guy always wins" is that it is not always true.

The term "faith tradition" seems most accurate as the root for my values. Founding my discussion of the source of my values in terms of "faith traditions" is productive for several reasons. First, many of the values I hold—such as a fundamental respect for all people, conceptions of justice and fairness, and ideas of stewardship—are also shared by other faiths like Islam and Judaism.

"Faith tradition" is also personal enough that I can hold a longer, more meaningful conversation about the source of my ethics by using it. Finally, using the term "faith tradition" does not shy away from talk of my belief system, but at the same time may help avoid unproductive discussions of religious systems in general. Like many, I am reticent to identify myself as a fervently religious person; I see the Christian faith as more about a relationship with God than strict adherence to religious customs and practices (although this in no way diminishes the importance of following biblical principles).

What will I do to stay ethically fresh?

David Miller in his book *God at Work* describes people who "feel an urgent need to integrate their faith and their work and, at the same time, have found the church to be of little help" (p. 9). I am one of those people.

Recently, I heard a sermon in which the pastor listed ministry possibilities: leading a small group, working to prepare the building for Sunday service, singing in the choir, serving as an elder or a deacon. He made no mention of how I might go about, or if I even could, "minister" in my cubicle where I spend the largest part of my waking time during the week. Later, the preacher prayed that the Lord would give us guidance as to whether our ministry was part-time or full-time. Again, the suggestion here was that ministry is something done only at church.

The implication was that those of us who earn our living outside this ordained path can have a part-time ministry serving as greeters, choir members, and/or church officers. During this message, I realized that in order to stay ethically fresh, particularly as I walk through the business world, I would not be able to rely fully on my church.

While institutional support may not be completely present, my church and the people who attend it will still be a resource for me, particularly as I seek to avoid ethical pitfalls both in my career and in my life. Many others are present in the church who are living and working in similar environments, striving for spiritual success in a largely material world just as I am. To create the proper ethical support network, it would be helpful to seek out the perspective of many different types of people within the church, even those that may have a more narrow view of what is and is not ministry.

Staying ethically fresh means spending significant time with those who do not have such a polarized view of work and faith. I need those who realize that I need encouragement as I seek to have a full-time ministry at home and work as well as when I walk into the doors of our church. The *Believers in Business Conference*, an annual gathering of students and professionals who are working through these same issues, has been a great source of encouragement in this effort. To stay ethically fresh I will seek to attend similar conferences and explore related resources as often as I can.

The teachings of the Bible and my guiding ethical principles are intricately connected. Therefore, to stay ethically fresh I need to spend regular time studying the Bible and learning how its principles relate to business. I am reminded of two speakers at the *2008 Believers in Business Conference*. One, a senior executive in the packaged goods industry, challenges himself to read a different translation of the Bible, cover-to-cover, every year. Another, a senior executive in the banking industry, has made a commitment that he will not leave the house in the morning without "putting on the armor of God" by spending time in the Bible. That these two individuals have made time for this activity reinforces the idea, for me, that to stay ethically fresh I must continually seek to learn more of what my own faith tradition teaches about business life straight from its source.

what is your greatest ethical dilemma?

join the conversation at
www.oursoulsatwork.com/ethics

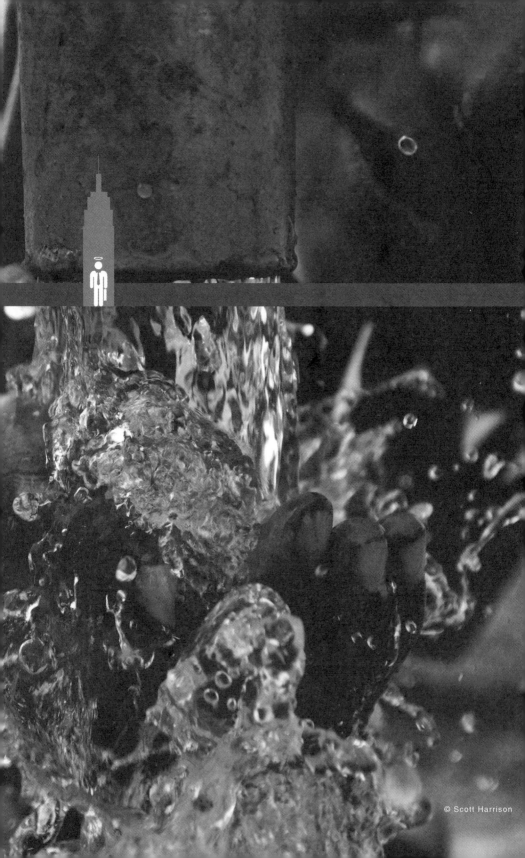

© Scott Harrison

CHAPTER TWELVE
GIVING

"If anyone gives even a cup of cold water to one of these little ones because he is my disciple, I tell you the truth, he will certainly not lose his reward."

Matthew 10:42

The argument of much of this book has been that business should operate in an ethical and responsible manner, and if business functions in this way, then it will serve the citizens of the world by effectively meeting their needs. Business, properly carried out, can be a tremendous power for good. However, there is one more topic we should consider when reflecting upon its positive potential; namely, there is a time and a place for businesses to give back to the communities they serve. This, of course, helps a business financially over the long term—a stronger community is able to purchase more goods and services—but giving at its spiritual core is about doing the right thing and not about the potential benefits that will flow back from the act.

The perfect "sweet spot" is when the needs of society intersect with the needs of the business. This is truly a "win-win" scenario for both parties. Engaged businesses are not only capable of helping communities develop socially and economically, but responsive communities strengthen a business's "license to operate," which is critically important for long-term success. In short, the recipe is seemingly simple, yet challenging to implement: Start with a spiritual foundation of ethics and morality, then determine what would best suit communities, the greater good of society, and yes—the interests of the business.

Giving, particularly for companies, is frequently only thought of in terms of philanthropy: giving cash to various humanitarian organizations. In some ways, this traditional approach to philanthropy is changing, thanks to people like Bill and Melinda Gates, and so many others who are catalyzing the revolution of "smart philanthropy" or "hands on philanthropy."

In this model, certainly the funding is still important, but there are also other elements involved—capability building, knowledge transfer, employee volunteerism, and strategic guidance. For companies, giving can be manifest through the use of their facilities and other resources during times of extreme need. Companies can allow employees to donate part of their paid time to local nonprofit agencies. Companies can also consult in their area of expertise for community development organizations, which often need it desperately!

The emerging social consciousness in business has caused many companies to look seriously and comprehensively at their environmental and community impact to find innovative solutions to societal problems on various different levels. There is a developing trend of public/private partnerships between for-profit business, academia, non-governmental nonprofit organizations, and governmental organizations that is commonly referred to as "collaborative social responsibility."

The bottom line—and, in fact, perhaps one of the core messages of this chapter—is that no one can do it alone. No single sector of society, not the government, not the humanitarian organizations, and not even multinational corporations, will be effective without the help of those in the other spheres as well. To create far-reaching sustainable change, we need to see an increase in collaborative innovation between the private sector (business), the public sector (governments), the social sector (humanitarian and mission organizations), academia (to assure evidence-based approaches to global challenges), and individuals.

There are undoubtedly numerous global problems that deserve tremendous attention, but it is hard to find something more fundamental to our survival and flourishing than clean drinking water. Without it, we die. Without good and normal access to it, humans all over the world spend most of our lives anemic and sick and struggle from one day to the next.

If there is anything that is deserving of an all hands on deck approach, it is the global movement for clean drinking water for everyone, everywhere. In fact, no other single natural element sits at the nexus of so many challenges—global health, hunger (through food security and agriculture), spirituality (for example, the importance of the Ganges to Hinduism), gender empowerment, (since in developing economies, it is often the young girls who are forced to miss school to walk six hours a day to fetch water) and education. Clearly, water deserves attention.

Community development practitioners have long recognized the desperate need for clean drinking water in various parts of the world. However, they are frequently like the John the Baptists of the world—voices crying out in the wilderness—who, unfortunately, are easily ignored by the fast moving train of the global economy. Thankfully, the facts that real change is needed and that business can play a significant role, are being recognized by many of the world's greatest companies, particularly Coca-Cola and PepsiCo.

————————————————

Coca-Cola :
WATER AND SYSTEMS IN TIMES OF DISASTER

The Coca-Cola Company recognizes that it is in a unique position to provide assistance during and after natural disasters. As a result of their exceptionally large distribution network, they can deliver necessities quickly and efficiently. Within hours of the terrorist attack on the World Trade Center, Coca Cola donated $12 million, scores of truckloads of water and juice, and hundreds of volunteers to support the rescue and recovery effort in New York and Washington, DC.

Following the tsunami disaster in December 2004, Coca-Cola and its bottling partners quickly contributed clean drinking water and provided sustained support to large-scale relief and reconstruction efforts. Knowing it takes a long time to recover from a disaster and that water is core to that recovery, Coca-Cola committed to staying involved for the long haul with an emphasis on helping reconstruct community water and sanitation needs.

Working in collaboration with the United Nations Development Programme (UNDP), Coca Cola also helped in remote, tsunami-hit areas of Indonesia, Sri Lanka, the Maldives, and Thailand to expand community access to clean drinking water. For example, with partners, Coca-Cola helped enable long-term provision of a water supply and public sanitation to some of the still-affected villages in Aceh, Indonesia. This program is providing water and promoting long-term hygiene and sanitation awareness to an estimated 7,000 villagers.

Traditional corporate philanthropy is generally a cash donation. However, this project exceeds that traditional model by harnessing the Coca-Cola system's non-cash resources, skills, and competencies. For example, in addition to donating water to the Red Cross immediately following the tsunami, Coca-Cola employees contributed to the rebuilding process on company time, including up to one-year assignments at partner organizations. Collaborative social responsibility among entities from various sectors continues to be crucial in the tsunami rebuilding process.

This was not a one-time thing for Coca-Cola. In 2007, flooding swept two states in Mexico, leaving residents without shelter, food, water, and clothing. Coca-Cola donated 1.5 million liters of bottled water and beverages, medicine and basic supplies, tents for temporary shelter; and the use of their distribution center for delivery of these much-needed supplies.

PepsiCo:
COMMUNITY DEVELOPMENT THROUGH
WATER PURIFICATION[1]

In May of 2009, PepsiCo became one of the first companies of its size to formally and publicly recognize water as a fundamental human right. While this is intuitive to most, it can be catalyzing for a company of PepsiCo's size to make such a visible statement. PepsiCo went beyond what is merely intuitive and established a Human Right to Water Policy in support of the United Nations/World Health Organization's document on the subject. But PepsiCo's water stewardship efforts had been robust long before their commitment in May of 2009.

In November 2007 I went to Manila, Philippines, on a consulting trip for a microfinance organization. As a part of my research, I was taken to a very large slum for a microfinance group meeting. On the way through the slum, I noticed a large and beautiful water purification system. Its well-organized and very clean appearance stood out from the dirty and difficult setting of the slum.

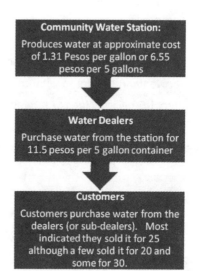

Community Water Station:
Produces water at approximate cost of 1.31 Pesos per gallon or 6.55 pesos per 5 gallons

Water Dealers
Purchase water from the station for 11.5 pesos per 5 gallon container

Customers
Customers purchase water from the dealers (or sub-dealers). Most indicated they sold it for 25 although a few sold it for 20 and some for 30.

As I asked questions, I learned that the purification system was the result of a partnership between PepsiCo and the Wholistic Transformation Resource Centre (WTRC) carried out in cooperation with my host, the

---

1   The graphs and data collected in this section were used by permission from Brown, Michelle, 2009. "Strategies and approaches for understanding impact at the base of the pyramid: a review of approaches and early lessons from a Community Water Project in the Philippines." Working draft of article currently being finalized for publication and part of authors PhD research at the University of Hong Kong.

Centre for Community Transformation (CCT). Prior to the project, local residents suffered from either a lack of access to clean drinking water or exorbitant prices for clean water from local water distributors.

Through their participation in the project, PepsiCo helped to offset both of these problems: by first increasing people's access to clean drinking water, and then by partnering with a socially minded humanitarian organization, they ensured that the resulting consumer prices would not be inappropriate for the context.

PepsiCo supported the project through financial contributions and consulting services, even at the executive level. The PepsiCo CFO of the Philippines visited the site in early 2009 and consulted regarded pricing and the project's financing.

The three partners are now managing to leverage the water station in numerous ways. The water is put into five-gallon containers and delivered by water dealers who typically carry six at a time in a specially designed cart attached to their bicycle. CCT recruits the water dealers from among the homeless. Not only are local residents getting drinking water at affordable rates, but the project also employs the unemployed which produces necessary income for more dignified housing, not to mention a more dignified life.

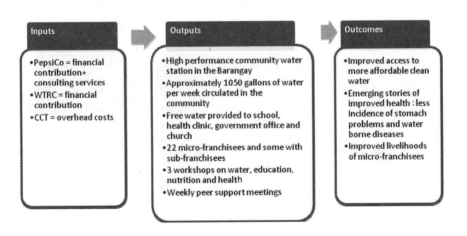

Inputs
- PepsiCo = financial contribution + consulting services
- WTRC = financial contribution
- CCT = overhead costs

Outputs
- High performance community water station in the Barangay
- Approximately 1050 gallons of water per week circulated in the community
- Free water provided to school, health clinic, government office and church
- 22 micro-franchisees and some with sub-franchisees
- 3 workshops on water, education, nutrition and health
- Weekly peer support meetings

Outcomes
- Improved access to more affordable clean water
- Emerging stories of improved health : less incidence of stomach problems and water borne diseases
- Improved livelihoods of micro-franchisees

In just a little more than a year, the project yielded the following results:

- Water was sold to communities at a price fifty percent less than had been previously available (as low as US $0.25/five gallon container)
- Sixty-four individuals established water-related businesses serving approximately 1,000 households, or at least 5,000 individuals
- It generated a modest profit
- The community center was used for dealership meetings, health education seminars, and services for local churches
- The center also gave a place to display and sell CCT's microfinance services, as well as affordable generic medical products.

Remember earlier in this chapter, we introduced the idea of "sweet spot" or the "perfect marriage" between business and community needs? The PepsiCo model in the Philippines is one example of this at work, and one which was personally experienced and can be attested to by the author!

DOING IT THE RIGHT WAY
at Coca-Cola

Critics of large corporations frequently say that these companies cover up their damaging actions through community development or disaster relief initiatives. Regardless of how often that is true, at the end of the day, in everything they do, businesses have to be doing it in the right way.

Recognizing this, former Coca Cola Chairman and CEO, E. Neville Isdell, announced a corporate vision of returning back to nature an amount of water equal to what they use in all of their beverages and their production by 2020. Accomplishing this will take an intentional and comprehensive strategy. At Coca Cola this means reducing the amount of water used to produce beverages, recycling water used for manufacturing processes so it can be returned safely to the environment, and replenishing water in communities and nature through locally relevant projects.

Forty percent of the water Coca-Cola uses globally goes into their finished products, while the remaining sixty percent is used in the beverage manufacturing process for rinsing, cleaning, and cooling. Despite the fact that Coca-Cola products have grown more than fifteen percent since 2002, their water consumption has actually declined by nineteen percent.

Coca-Cola has made a very public pledge to continue to improve their water-saving measures until they replace, drop for drop, all of the water they use in their operations—and has initiated partnerships in many developing countries to establish local rainwater harvesting and to provide accessible fresh and clean water in rural villages. The women in these villages, who used to walk many miles every day for clean water, now have up to an extra six hours each day. With this extra time, they've started their own small businesses in order to improve the well-being of their families and their communities. They're simply living out the reality of the critical role of business right in their own communities.

DOING IT THE RIGHT WAY
at PepsiCo

Steve Reinemund's replacement, PepsiCo CEO and Chairman Indra K. Nooyi, has said,

> *Performance with purpose is at the foundation of every aspect of our business. Indeed, financial achievement can and must go hand-in-hand with sustainability. We integrate a commitment to human, environmental, and talent sustainability into all of our operations. Doing so creates a blueprint for PepsiCo to develop, manufacture, and sell our*

products in a sustainable way, gives us a competitive advantage in markets all over the world, which in turn drives long-term growth. [2]

PepsiCo also recognizes that water is an enormous issue and one which everyone, themselves included, must take seriously. Dan Bena, Director of Sustainability and Environmental Health Systems at PepsiCo, notes that water, more than most things, fits the triple bottom line well—sitting squarely at the nexus of water security, food security, and global health.

Climate Change
Dramatic increase in severity of floods that adversely impact poor coastal communities

Water Scarcity
Already 1.2 billion people—twenty percent of world's population—lack clean drinking water

Unrelenting Hunger and Food Security
Drought exacerbates the chronic hunger facing more than 1 billion worldwide

Sanitation and Health
2.6 billion people lack access to sanitation; in developing economies, ninety to ninety-five percent of sewage and seventy percent of industrial wastes is dumped into and pollutes the local water supply

Abject Poverty and Gender Inequality
600 million children live in households earning less than $1 a day—more than half of them are girls

In order to ensure that they are doing it the right way, as introduced earlier in this chapter, PepsiCo has adopted the following Human Right to Water Policy, which has established the following guidelines:

• Safety: PepsiCo will ensure that their operations preserve the quality of the water resources in the communities in which they do business;

• Sufficiency: Their operating objective is to ensure that their use of water will not diminish the availability of community water resources to the individuals or the communities in the areas in which they operate;

2 Provided by Dan Bena, Director of Sustainability and Environmental Health Systems at PepsiCo via personal correspondence

- Acceptability: They will involve communities in their plans to develop water resources and will assure transparency of any risks or challenges to the local governments and community members in an on-going manner;

- Physical Accessibility: They will assure that their operations will not adversely impact physical accessibility of community members to community water resources and will address community concerns in a cooperative manner;

- Affordability: They will appropriately advocate to applicable government bodies that safe water supplies should be available in a fair and equitable manner to members of the community. Such water should be safe and of consistent and adequate supply and affordable within local practices.

Being intentional regarding water efficiency helps. In 2008, PepsiCo conserved more than 7.5 billion liters of water as a result of gains in water efficiency. At PepsiCo, water responsibly is a top priority, but they also recognize their ability to help address the broader challenge of water scarcity and to help avoid water conflicts in local communities. While traditional philanthropy is still so important and necessary, businesses can significantly and positively contribute to global solutions by looking innovatively at new models—ways to preserve the dignity of the people that need help the most—that not only provide the "fish," but also teach them the skills to "fish" for themselves!

UN CEO WATER MANDATE

PepsiCo and Coca-Cola have joined the UN CEO Water Mandate, which is an "initiative designed to assist companies in the development, implementation, and disclosure of water sustainability policies and practices." [3] Dan Bena, Director of Sustainability at PepsiCo and its representative to the Mandate, says, "The

3   "The CEO Water Mandate," United Nations Global Compact website, http://www.unglobalcompact.org/Issues/Environment/CEO_Water_Mandate.

CEO Water Mandate is perhaps the single most succinct and holistic vehicle to capture how the private sector can partner with other interested parties to help mitigate and adapt to the global water crises."[4]

The 2006 Human Development Report states: "The global crisis in water consigns large segments of humanity to lives of poverty, vulnerability, and insecurity." Water is core to human life and our ability to love, share, care, succeed, work, and everything else.

One billion people are denied the right to clean water and 2.6 billion people lack access to adequate sanitation. We can become numb to such large numbers. Personalize this by meditating on the fact that a child dies every fifteen seconds from a water-related illness, generally diarrhea—*every fifteen seconds*. It probably took you longer than that to read this paragraph. Perhaps even more unconscionable than this fact alone, is that a large percentage of these deaths—some say as many as eighty percent—can be prevented with simple re-hydration techniques.

At the end of the day, there is an overwhelming need for us to give generously of our time, skills, and finances. Not only for the development of the common good, but for the growth of our own souls. It was Jesus who said, "From everyone who has been given much, much will be demanded; and from the one who has been entrusted with much, much more will be asked" (Luke 12:48).

SCOTT HARRISON on
THE STORY OF charity : water (bio p. 256)

When I was four years old, my conservative Christian parents and I moved from our home in Philadelphia to an "energy efficient" home in New Jersey. Unfortunately, not even the inspectors noticed the four quarter-sized cracks in our gas

---

4   Personal Correspondence.

furnace. While my dad was working and commuting, and I was outside playing with friends, my mom was in our home breathing carbon monoxide day in and day out. Finally, she collapsed and was rushed to the hospital with carbon monoxide poisoning. It was too late to reverse the damage. Mom went from a healthy young woman to an invalid whose immune system saw all chemicals as the enemy. For the rest of her days, she was allergic to anything chemically based.

Moving forward to my teenage years, I was the ideal Christian son, active in youth groups and Bible study, pretty good in school, no problem to my parents, helping with Mom's care. Home life was unusual. My mom basically lived in our tile bathroom with foil on the door to keep out the fumes of the stain that had been used on the door five years earlier. To talk with her face to face, we had to go out into the yard and I had to stand downwind so no chemicals from my clothes, etc. would reach her. My clothes had to be washed in baking soda. Life revolved around providing a toxin-free environment for my mother.

At eighteen, I joined a rock band and moved to New York City to become rich and famous and rebelled against the disciplines of my faith. I wanted to do everything I had been told I couldn't do. I dove deeply into the New York nightlife. Our band was talented musically, but challenged relationally, and we eventually split up. I noticed that the guy who regularly booked our band worked very little and made lots of money. I liked that combination and figured I could pull it off. I began working at a club called Mel's on 14th Street. We were successful in promoting a high level R&B open mic night, pulling in folks like Stevie Wonder and Prince. Many incredible singers came through the club.

During the few years I worked at Mel's, I went to college part time. I didn't live on campus and gave college just enough effort to make my dad happy, barely pulling *Cs* in my classes. Our promoting services morphed from Mel's R&B scene to the fashion world at a club just around the corner from my apartment. Models, celebrities, and stars were drawn to this club. Soon, I was being paid $2,000 a month to drink Bacardi products at the club and Budweiser also paid me nearly $2,000 a month to down Bud during parties. Ironically, we were considered "influencers" when we were actually just people who partied hard. The clubs were high end, selling $300 bottles of vodka and $15 drinks.

Almost a decade into this life, I began to feel numbness and tingling in my arm and submitted myself to a battery of tests for MS, Parkinson's, diabetes, and anything else the doctors could think of. Though they found nothing wrong and the tingling went away, I was suddenly touched by my own mortality. A few months later, a group of my partying friends, my girlfriend at the time, and I rented a gorgeous house in Uruguay for a month. It was the perfect place for God to get my attention. I would party 'til five in the morning, and then read A.W. Tozer and the Bible all afternoon. A push-pull for my soul had begun.

I realized I had become the most selfish, arrogant, miserable person I knew. Many of the people around me weren't exhibiting the values of my faith, which I'd covered up but still held deep down inside of me. I hadn't yet become an atheist and completely walked away from my faith. I had simply walked away from obedience—very, very, very far away into a small corner—but my faith was still there. During that vacation, I resolved to come back and live life differently, which was a challenge since I didn't know how to do anything other than what I had been doing the last ten years!

Back in New York City I floundered. I stopped doing drugs and tried to drink less, but wasn't very successful. Four months later, something happened in one of the clubs that made me see nightclub life for what is was. So I took a month off and went north to New Hampshire and Maine with my Bible in an effort to figure out what the Bible was saying to me personally. It dawned on me I did not have to go back to New York. I could do something radically different. After praying and searching and thinking, I decided, "Wouldn't it be cool if I made my life look just the opposite—serve God and the poor instead of only myself?" I got the dream to go to the poorest country in the world and serve the people there. The challenge was finding a Christian organization that would take me. Having a nightclub promoter on your roster was not what most mission groups were looking for.

So, I didn't go back to New York. Instead, I continued my search while staying with a friend in France. One group really struck me as "out there." They were called Mercy Ships. These served as floating hospitals for doctors and surgeons who used their vacations to fly to the poorest countries in the world and volunteer their time aboard a 500-foot long yacht remodeled into a medical center where they would operate on and give medical attention to the world's poor. Staff volunteers paid $500 a month to serve aboard the Mercy Ships. This definitely fit into the "opposite" box of the way I had formerly lived.

I applied for the only open position: photographer. I had no photography training but put together a nice portfolio of pieces from vacations, life, portraits, etc. With my "credentials," I didn't receive a positive response to my application, but as the photographer position remained open and the sailing date came closer, Mercy Ships contacted me in the south of France and asked me to meet them in Germany. They were very clear, "We aren't agreeing to take you. We are only agreeing to *meet* you." I needed to convince them that I wasn't crazy, I wasn't going to throw raves or otherwise corrupt the crew, and that I really wanted to serve God and the poor. A few weeks later, I was on the ship in our first port: Benin, West Africa. Our ultimate destination was Liberia, a country destroyed by war.

For eight months, my job was to photograph everything that happened on board the ships and out in the villages. On our third day, I looked onto the docks and saw 5,000 people lined up in hopes of becoming one of the 1,500 patients our doctors could care for. One fourteen-year-old boy, Alfred, overwhelmed my senses. There on the other side of my lens was a teenager with a face totally disfigured by a fourteen-pound tumor that was slowly suffocating him. His eyes radiated anger. I fell apart and had to find a corner to collect myself. The ship's medical director told me I'd see much more of that, but that Alfred's story would end well. And it did. Three weeks later I got to take Alfred back to his village. Today he is a strong, normal, happy young man.

I also got to witness thirty-year-old women blinded by cataracts precipitated by their traditional equatorial sun dancing, clapping, and able to see just one day after cataract surgery. Day after day the stories mounted.

It was during this time I began to understand issues around water. The Mercy Ships approach was, "We've got 300 volunteers. Let's make the greatest difference we can." So we went out to the villages to see what we could do. One of my best friends was a water engineer. Leif dug five or six wells a year. I was struck by the incredible impact a few thousand dollars could make when used to dig a simple well. A village of several hundred people could drink pure water instead of drinking from a disease-infested swamp. I learned eighty percent of disease on our planet is in some way related to unsafe water, lack of sanitation, or polluted water.

After nearly a year, I flew home and within an hour of landing in New York, I was back up on a rooftop patio with a $16 margarita in my hand. My two worlds collided. Here I was holding in my hand a drink that cost as much as a bag of rice which would feed a family of four for a month in Liberia. It was too much.

The next couple months I ran around with my laptop telling the stories of the people whose lives were changed on the Mercy Ships. The Mercy Ships were virtually unknown, and I wanted people to hear about their work. The idea for an exhibition dawned on me. I was given space in a gallery and did an eight-day exhibition of the photos I'd taken during the previous voyage. People came, and we raised $95,000, which all went to the Mercy Ships organization.

But what was I going to do with my life after that? I decided to "follow the money." I went back to Mercy Ships to photograph what the $95,000 accomplished. I sailed with Mercy Ships for another year, following the medical work, and digging more water wells. After I wrapped up my two-year tour with Mercy Ships, I returned to New York and again faced the decision: What would I do with my life? I knew I would be doing work with the poorest of the poor for the rest of my life, but my vision was a bit larger than Mercy Ships. I wanted to do something radically innovative, something that would have incredible impact.

At the same time, a lot of my friends were disenchanted with "charity" because most believed that only ten percent of what people give ever gets to those who need it. I saw an incredible opportunity to bring a large group of people back to the table, but we needed to reinvent charity and we needed to choose the issue of focus.

Water seemed the one issue that touched everything. Health is not the only thing affected by water. Women walking three hours each way to get a jerry can of muddy water have no time to build a micro-business or in any other way contribute to family funds. Girls lose their chance at education because they must spend their time collecting water for their families. Children miss months and years of school due to water-related illnesses. Health, economics, and education are all impacted by the shortage of safe water resources around the world. More than a billion people do not have access to safe drinking water. We wanted to reinvent charity, and we were all about water. What better name to give our group than "charity: water."

Nightclub promoters make a lot of money on their birthdays. They throw a big fling; then people come and buy their drinks. It's a lucrative night. We launched charity: water on my birthday, September 7, 2006, in a new club that had not yet opened. Seven hundred people came, paid $20, got a tour of the new club, and helped start charity: water. The $15,000 raised that night went to build six wells in northern Uganda. Every penny went straight to well digging. Charity: water was on the way!

Our one-hundred-percent model began that night. Every dollar donated for charity: water projects goes to clean water projects. Our administrative costs are paid from a totally different sector which donates specifically for that purpose. We felt if we were going to reinvent charity, it had to begin with what we did with the funds.

I went off to Uganda to work with local partners, photograph the sites before and after and provide living, real-time proof that our donors' dollars were making a difference. This has become another part of our business model. All our projects are equipped with GPS, cameras, and computers that are linked to Google Earth so that at any given time our donors can see what's happening at any project site.

Telling the stories has been our most important marketing tool. We want our website to be as compelling, edgy, and real—recognized as the best sites out there so that these stories can be seen and heard. The idea of giving your birthday for a well site and having folks bring $20 for charity: water has taken off and hundreds of thousands of dollars have been raised by people giving up birthdays, wedding gifts, even funeral donations. The first "Twestival" (or "Twitter-festival") was the brainchild of a friend of charity: water and was run totally independently by volunteers in various locations around the globe. We have done public service announcements (PSAs) and had films at the Sundance film festival. People can understand and see the impact of clean water sources through the stories we tell and that has grown our cause over and over again.

Choosing the countries in which we work is a matter of identifying the countries where water is scarce, ruling out countries at war because we don't have proficiencies for war zones, ruling out countries that don't want help, and then beginning to set up a working structure with countries, finding local help, and creating partnerships.

In the field, the work is done totally by local partners. We may interview three or four national companies that have been drilling wells, protecting springs, and/or creating bio-sand filters for ten to twelve years. We select the most exceptional company and begin to work with them, first on small projects and then expanding their projects and influence as our relationship grows. Some have now been responsible for over $5 million in projects.

When we have funds for one hundred wells and a need for five hundred, our local partners are the ones who look into the situation in each village—ground water, rainwater, current quality of the water, everything. They are the ones who triage the sites with the most needy and likely sites coming first.

Our five-year plan is to raise $200 million to reach ten million people. That's just a tiny percentage of the 1.1 billion without safe water, but it's a start. We believe we can provide safe drinking water to every person on the planet in our lifetime. It's certainly a goal worth giving my life to and I can't imagine ever doing anything else.

how can we change the world through giving?

**join the conversation at
www.oursoulsatwork.com/giving**

OUR SOULS AT WORK

AFTERWORD

BY MARK L RUSSELL

AFTERWORD

The world's best businesses have not yet been built. And we are the ones who can build them. An emerging generation of business builders exists among us, and through our God given ingenuity, we can build businesses that meet more needs, serve more people, and produce more human flourishing and well-being than ever before.

This book has featured contributions from executives of world-class corporations like Coca-Cola, PepsiCo, and Tyson Foods, as well as emerging leaders of small and mid-size companies. There is no doubt in my mind that the best is yet to come, not only from the contributors of this book, but also from those who take these principles and values seriously, personalize them, and commit to living by them.

As humans, we are still capable of great things. We can find innovative solutions to the world's most serious problems. We can solve the clean water crisis. We can eradicate extreme poverty and we can live happy and fulfilling balanced lives as husbands, wives, fathers, mothers, churchgoers, and community citizens.

Work is not the chief purpose of our lives, but there is a purpose for it. Business is not the only means to solving the world's problems, but it has to be a significant player in the game. Moving into the future, it is imperative that we understand the divine purposes for business and for our work. This will enable us to prosper holistically and honorably.

This book is just a beginning. As we go into all the world, following Christ and doing our jobs, may we live our own stories as leaders of faith in the global marketplace—may we live in relationship with one another, reflecting God's truth, and sharing our failures and our successes so that at the end of the day we can say with confidence, "I have fought the good fight, I have finished the race, I have kept the faith" (2 Timothy 4:7).

OUR SOULS AT WORK
ACKNOWLEDGEMENTS

ACKNOWLEDGEMENTS

Even single-author books are indebted to the work of several people. A book with thirty-seven contributors is produced by the work of people too numerous to name—but I'll try. First, I would like to thank all of the contributors who had no financial or other incentive to work with us, other than they believed in the cause, and wanted to help in any way they could. I have been humbled by their time, support, and attention to detail.

Susan Tilton deserves a special thanks for transcribing all of the talks. Andrea Nagy Smith and Nicole Wong organized and edited the material in such a way that demonstrated they are truly professionals. Sandi Funkhouser was coordinator extraordinaire and helped me to keep my sanity when I was neck deep in multiple projects. Drew Steffen is the genius behind the graphic development and helped me think through a variety of issues.

Many thanks are in order to Lynette Ryan and Dan Bena at PepsiCo for their last minute support in verifying important details.

The chapter 12 section of PepsiCo's work in the Philippines is particularly indebted to Michelle Brown, who graciously gave us permission to use her working draft of an article currently being finalized for publication and part of her PhD research at the University of Hong Kong.

I would also like to particularly acknowledge David Miller, whose intellect and insights have shaped and formed me. His leadership and vision were the positive force behind the Believers in Business Conferences.

My brother, Jeff Russell, has been a super help and encouragement through this entire process. I cannot overstate what an influence he has had on me.

Jeffrey Metzner, Kimberly Yerino, and Jaison Ipe of the Yale School of Management Christian Fellowship merit recognition for their support and logistical assistance in connecting and cooperating with the contributors. Rick Schneider of the Rivendell Institute, likewise, generously offered assistance when we needed it.

Most importantly, I want to give a special thanks to my wife, Laurie, who listened to me ramble on about this book way more than someone should have to and who never complained about my late nights working on it.

And to our children, Noah and Anastasia, may this book one day encourage you to live out your faith wherever you are and in everything you do.

OUR SOULS AT WORK
CONTRIBUTORS

CONTRIBUTORS

(listed alphabetically, with pages containing contributions)

MAX ANDERSON (107-113)

Max Anderson graduated with masters' degrees from the Harvard Business School and the Harvard Kennedy School in 2009. He has worked as a consultant at McKinsey, and has worked and studied theology at Redeemer Presbyterian Church in Manhattan. He now works in investment management and lives with his wife and daughter in New York City.

MO ANDERSON (81-87)

Strong, principled, and compassionate, Mo Anderson's personal integrity and un-ending drive are touchstones that have made Keller Williams Realty one of the most successful franchises in real estate history. She established her first real estate office, a Century 21 franchise, in Edmond, Oklahoma, in 1975; soon after, it was the third top-producing office out of 7,500 Century 21 locations in North America. In 1986 Mo sold her company to Merrill Lynch Realty, where she served as a district vice president until December 1989.

In 1992, Anderson became the first Keller Williams Realty franchisee outside of the state of Texas when she persuaded Gary Keller to expand his profit-share concept for real estate offices. She launched the Oklahoma region and became co-owner of two Keller Williams market centers in that state.

In January 1995, Anderson became president and CEO of Keller Williams Realty. Since 2005, Anderson has served as the vice chairman for the company. Her focus is on cultivating the unique culture of Keller Williams Realty.

Anderson founded KW Cares (501(c)(3) nonprofit organization) in 2002 to assist company associates and their families in need and raised millions for Hurricane Katrina relief. She has been named twice as Oklahoma's Women in Business Advocate of the Year by the U.S. Small Business Administration. In December

2006, Anderson was named one of *America's Top Twenty-five Influential Thought Leaders by REALTOR®* magazine. In January 2007, the Women's Council of REALTORS® featured her as one of *Real Estate's Most Influential People* in an article published in *Connections*. And, in 2008, Anderson was inducted into the prestigious *Hall of Leaders* by the CRB Council.

DENNIS BAKKE (23-26, 51-56, 60)

Dennis Bakke co-founded AES Corporation, a global electric company, in 1981 and was president and CEO from 1994 to 2002, during which time he built the international energy company into a multi-billion dollar enterprise with 40,000 employees in thirty-one countries. Currently, he is president and CEO of Imagine Schools, operating seventy elementary and secondary charter schools in ten states.

His innovative and often provocative bestselling book, *Joy at Work: A Revolutionary Approach to Fun on the Job*, tells the story of the transformation he watched in businesses, plants, and people as he put into practice the purpose of making AES the most fun place to work on the planet. One plant's experience, in the former Soviet Republic of Georgia, was documented in the film *Power Trip.*

COREY BELL (66-68)

Corey Bell is the CEO and co-founder of TriFusion. Before helping found TriFusion in October 2003, Corey was a supply chain manager for Dell Computer Corporation. He specializes in creating effective strategies that maximize channel effectiveness, asset management, personnel performance, and productivity. His experience with Centurion Holdings Group, a private equity venture investment group, National Biscuit Company (Nabisco), Chrysler Corporation, and Dell Computer Corporation has allowed him to work with some of the country's most distinguished and innovative brands. He finished his legal studies at the University of Texas School of Law, and his Master of Business Administration from the University of Tennessee.

SPENCER BRAND (73-76)

Spencer Brand is the Founder and President of The Endowment for Community Leadership, a nonprofit organization committed to developing ethnic Christian leadership in the major metropolitan areas of the United States. Spencer worked in the early 1970s as the Special Assistant to the Assistant Secretary for the U.S. Department of Labor and the Department of the Interior. He joined the staff of Campus Crusade for Christ in 1976 and has served as Director of Here's Life Washington and Associate National Director for Here's Life America. He currently serves as Director of Special Projects.

TEAL CARLOCK (107-113)

Teal Carlock works at Genentech in the San Francisco Bay Area. Previously he worked for ABF Freight System where he was lead pricing analyst. He holds a Bachelor of Science and Master of Science in Industrial Engineering from the University of Oklahoma, and a Master of Business Administration from Harvard Business School. He is an avid cyclist and runner and loves to spend time with his outstanding wife, Laren.

BEN CHATRAW (70-73)

Ben Chatraw is the co-founder of Vision Research Capital Management, LP, and Vision Research Organization, LLC, a Dallas-based investment manager for ac-credited and institutional investors. In his current role, Ben oversees all opera-tional activities involved in the day-to-day management of the firm.

Prior to founding Vision Research, Ben was a General Manager at Lucent Tech-nologies, where he was responsible for all supply chain activity supporting one of the company's largest customers. In this role he was accountable for complete supply cycle management and the delivery of over $150 million in equipment each quarter. Through his tenure at Lucent, Ben served as the youngest member of Lucent's strategic SCN Advisory Council. During his operating career, Ben also led the launch of a major marketplace initiative for a national nonprofit technology organization. He has held a diverse range of engineering, operating, and financial positions that have contributed to an expertise in developing and maintaining efficient and repeatable processes.

Ben is a graduate of the Georgia Institute of Technology where he was a President's Scholar and received a Bachelor of Industrial Engineering with highest honors. Ben holds a Master of Business Administration from Harvard Business School where he graduated with distinction.

The Chatraw family actively attends Brookhaven Church in Dallas, Texas, where Ben serves as a small group leader and as a member of the church's missions committee. He also serves as chairman of Videre Microfinance Institute, a Dallas-based ministry that has issued micro-loans to the working poor in Southern Sudan, and is an advisor to Southwest Good Samaritan Ministries.

HOWARD DAHL (26-27, 28-29, 54, 65, 68-69, 116, App. B)
Howard Dahl is the co-founder, President, and CEO of Amity Technology, a Fargo, North Dakota-based manufacturer of farm machinery. Its main product is sugar beet harvesting equipment, which dominates a majority of the U.S. market and is the primary leader in the Russian market. In 2007, Amity entered the air seeder market, which was the primary business of Concord, Incorporated, the company Howard led from 1977-1996. Amity is also the world's leading manufacturer of agricultural soil sampling equipment. Amity sells products in more than twenty-five different countries of the world. A sister company, Wil-Rich LLC, is a leading tillage manufacturer.

Howard is a Director of the Federal Reserve Board of Minneapolis and is a member of numerous other boards. Howard and his companies have been featured in national publications (like *Inc.* magazine) and are the recipients of a variety of awards such as North Dakota Exporter of the Year, 1994; North Dakota Innovator of the Year, 1997 (UND Center for Innovation); North Dakota Agricultural Person of the Year, 2004; Fargo-Moorhead Business of the Year, 2005; and First North Dakota company to be the SBA Region VII Exporter of the Year, 2006. Howard has a BS in Business Administration from the University of North Dakota and a

MA in Philosophy of Religion from Trinity Evangelical Divinity School. Howard and his wife, Ann, have three children.

KEN ELDRED (32-36, 114-116, 148-150, 159-160)
Ken Eldred founded many successful companies, including Ariba Technologies, Incorporated, the leader in the Internet business-to-business industry which has reached a market valuation of $40 billion; Inmac, which grew to $400 million in yearly revenues as the first business to sell computer products, supplies, and accessories by direct mail; Mysoftware Corporation, now called ClickAction; and Norm Thompson Outfitters, Incorporated, a direct mail, consumer specialty retailer of high-quality merchandise. In 1988, the Institute of American Entrepreneurs named Eldred "Retail Entrepreneur of the Year for the San Francisco Bay Area."

Eldred's book *God Is At Work: Transforming People and Nations Through Business* is a leading work in the movement to integrate faith and work. Eldred and his wife, Roberta, founded Living Stones Foundation, a public support organization created to support Christian work and charity around the world. He also serves as chairman of Parakletos@Ventures, a top-rated venture capital firm in the Silicon Valley, California.

Eldred, and his wife Roberta have three sons and currently reside in Silicon Valley.

KATHERINE FOO (102, 166-169, 181-182)
Born and raised in Maryland, Katherine Foo received her Bachelor of Arts in Biology from Columbia University, a Master of Public Health degree in Community Health Sciences from UCLA, and (as of December 2009) is a second-year Master of Business Administration student in Wharton's Health Care Management program. Katherine's professional experiences center around public health education and communications. She has worked at the Centers for Disease Control and Prevention in the areas of violence prevention and tuberculosis, as well as an HIV/AIDS community research organization, and a public health consulting

firm. She aspires to be involved in global health initiatives to increase access to medicines in developing countries.

DAVE GIBBONS (Foreword)

Dave Gibbons is a Xealot and Founding Partner of The Awaken Group (http://theawakengroup.com), a global leadership development/consulting firm with expertise in global culture, strategy, innovation, and creativity. He has a passion to see organizations and leaders have a double bottom line: to make a profit and make a difference. He also founded a nonprofit global leadership development and ideation group called XEALOT (http://xealot.net) connecting resources to marginalized leaders.

He is also the founding pastor of Newsong Church, an international multi-site church located in such places as Thailand, India, London, Los Angeles, Irvine, Dallas, Mexico City, and Beijing. Newsong is considered one of the most innovative churches in America by *Outreach* Magazine. Dave also serves on the Board of World Vision U.S. The author of *The Monkey and the Fish*, Gibbons is a vision-oriented leader known for his insightful thinking on the future of organizations.

BONITA GRUBBS (170-171)

Bonita Grubbs has been Executive Director of Christian Community Action since December 1988. Prior to that, she was employed as Assistant Regional Administrator within the State of Connecticut for the Department of Mental Health.

Rev. Grubbs currently serves in a leadership capacity on numerous boards and councils including the Fighting Back Project; Mercy Center in Madison, Connecticut; Connecticut Center for School Change and Dwight Hall at Yale University; the Connecticut Voices for Children; the Connecticut Housing Coalition; the Community Economic Development Fund; and the Hospital of St. Raphael, where she serves as Chairperson of its Mission Effectiveness Committee. She has also served as a lecturer in Homiletics at Yale Divinity School.

Rev. Grubbs holds an undergraduate degree in Sociology and Afro-American Studies from Smith College in Northampton, Massachusetts. She received two degrees from Yale University—a Master of Arts in Religion and a Master of Public Health. She received an honorary degree from Albertus Magnus College in 2001. In 1987, she was ordained through the American Baptist Church.

SCOTT HARRISON (147, 232-239)

In 2004, Scott Harrison left the streets of New York City for the shores of West Africa. For ten years, Harrison had made his living in the Big Apple promoting top nightclubs and fashion events, and for the most part living selfishly and arrogantly. He returned to his faith and chose to turn his life around by working with Mercy Ships as a photographer. After serving on the Mercy Ships, primarily in Liberia, Scott returned to New York and, in September 2006, founded charity: water, a nonprofit organization bringing clean and safe drinking water to people in developing nations.

In their first three years, charity: water has funded 1,549 projects in 16 countries, serving over 820,000 people. Learn more at www.charitywater.org.

HENRY KAESTNER (91-92, 139-141)

Kaestner joined Morken as Co-founder in 2001 when he merged Bandwidth International into Bandwidth.com and served as CEO until early 2008. In his position as Executive Chairman, Henry Kaestner works with partner David Morken on the firm's strategy, financing, and marketing functions. Kaestner also oversees the partnership's not-for-profit activities.

Previously, Kaestner was the CEO of Bandwidth International, an international wholesale telecommunications broker based in London, England. He also founded Chapel Hill Broadband. Kaestner was a founder and former President and CEO of Chapel Hill Brokers, an energy broker which achieved more than $50 million in daily trade volume on more than 150 transactions, for clients including Morgan Stanley and Merrill Lynch.

Together with business and ministry partner, David Morken, Henry has founded DurhamCares.org, an organization that seeks to engage residents of Durham and encourage them to immerse themselves in service to their city; and MinistrySpot-light.org, which seeks to identify best of breed, independent Christ-centered word and deed ministries around the globe.

Kaestner lives in Durham with his wife Kimberley and their three sons.

GEORGE F KETTLE (73-76)

George F. Kettle, a native Washingtonian, was well known in the Washington, DC, area as a successful businessman and philanthropist. He was honored as Washingtonian of the Year and Entrepreneur of the Year.

Mr. Kettle started his real estate brokerage office in 1965. In February 1973, he purchased the Century 21 master franchise for Virginia, Maryland, Washington, DC, Delaware, and Eastern Pennsylvania. In 1996, when he sold the franchises to HFS, Incorporated, he had over 430 offices and 6,000 sales associates.

Mr. Kettle brought the I Have a Dream program to Washington. He helped more than ninety students from the inner city with their college education and recruited more than a dozen other sponsors in cities across America. He devoted many hours to the Youth for Tomorrow Home for troubled teenagers, Calvin Wood-land's work with the inner city children of Washington, DC, and with Campus Crusade for Christ, Prison Fellowship Ministries, and The Endowment for Community Leadership. As well as his many contributions on a national level, Mr. Kettle was also deeply involved in meeting needs in Russia and Africa.

Mr. Kettle passed away April 15, 2009.

BLAKE LINGLE (127-130)

Blake Lingle is the CEO of the Boise Fry Company. After spending many moons slaving for Uncle Sam, Blake left civil service to flip burgers at Boise Fry Company. Some call his fry and burger making skills ninja-like, others call his skills overrated—depends on whom you ask. When Blake isn't making delicious fries and burgers, he's questioning why squirrels can't be pets, listening to Christmas music, playing Tetris, and/or chilling with his beautiful wife, Andrea. Blake's belief in God and miracles was confirmed when Andrea agreed to marry him. Blake and Andrea live in Boise, Idaho, with their golden retriever aptly named Chase.

BRIAN LEWIS (87-91)

Brian J. Lewis is Managing Partner of Cereus Partners, an advisory firm to corporations and philanthropic organizations in the areas of strategy, marketing focus, and message. A graduate of Fuller Theological Seminary, Mr. Lewis also serves on the board of HOPE International, a global microfinance organization.

A frequent public speaker, he lives with his wife Barbara on Orcas Island, Washington.

STEVE LYNN (69-70, 96-101, 118, 147, 160-162)

Steve Lynn is majority owner and Chairman of Cummings Incorporated and CEO of Back Yard Burgers, Inc. He served as CEO of Shoney's Incorporated from 1995-1998, and Sonic Corporation from 1983-1995. Lynn is known for transforming Sonic from a declining fast-food chain to the nation's largest chain of drive-in restaurants, with almost $2 billion in annual sales. His steadfast belief in putting value first has allowed him to develop positive work environments wherever he has held a leadership position.

Lynn has served on numerous boards including the Oklahoma City Chamber of Commerce, Oklahoma State Chamber of Commerce (past chairman), The Salvation Army, Fellowship of Christian Athletes, Young Presidents' Organization (past chairman), Oklahoma Baptist Medical Center, the University of Louisville, The

National Cowboy Hall of Fame, and the International Franchise Association. He and his wife, Milah, have been married for over thirty years.

MATTHEW McCREIGHT (163-164, 193-195)

Matthew McCreight is a managing partner at Robert H. Shaffer & Associates, LLC (RHS&A). He has been with the firm since the late 1980s, consulting with a wide variety of organizations across all sectors, including health care and manufacturing companies, financial service firms, governmental agencies, and nonprofits. For the past fifty years, RHS&A has been at the forefront of helping organizations carry out major strategic and operational changes in ways that generate significant improvements in business results. Recently the firm launched the nonprofit Rapid Results Institute, to apply this approach to transform the impact of large-scale development efforts in Africa.

Before joining RHS&A, Matthew earned his Bachelor of Arts in Economics from Wesleyan University, and his Master of Business Administration from the Yale School of Management. Matthew also serves on the board of the Overseas Ministry Study Center.

Matthew's wife, the Reverend Dr. Kathryn Greene-McCreight, is an Episcopal Priest and noted author. Matthew and Kathryn have two almost-grown children, Noah and Grace.

EDWIN MEESE III (31, 59-61, 117, 160, 175-177, 178-181, 183-184)

Edwin Meese III, the seventy-fifth Attorney General of the United States of America, is a prominent leader, thinker, and elder statesman in the conservative movement. Mr. Meese holds the Ronald Reagan Chair in Public Policy at The Heritage Foundation and is the Chairman of Heritage's Center for Legal and Judicial Studies.

Mr. Meese spent most of his adult life working with Governor and then President Ronald Reagan. He served as the seventy-fifth Attorney General of the United

States from February 1985 to August 1988. In 1985, he received the *Government Executive* magazine's annual award for excellence in management.

From 1977 to 1981, he was a Professor of Law at the University of San Diego, where he also was Director of the Center for Criminal Justice Policy and Management. Mr. Meese also served as Vice President for administration of Rohr Industries, Inc. in Chula Vista, California.

Mr. Meese graduated from Yale University in 1953 and holds a law degree from the University of California-Berkeley. He is a retired Colonel in the Army Reserve and remains active in numerous civic and educational organizations. He is the author or co-author of three books: *Leadership, Ethics and Policing; Making America Safer;* and *With Reagan: The Inside Story.* Mr. Meese and his wife, Ursula, have two grown children. They live in McLean, Virginia.

JEFFREY METZNER (212-219)

Jeff works in brand management at Procter & Gamble in Cincinnati, Ohio. Jeff earned his Master of Business Administration in 2008 from the Yale School of Management. While at Yale, he had the privilege of planning the 2008 Believers in Business Conference. Prior to matriculating at Yale, Jeff worked in residential construction as a project manager at Ryan Homes in Delaware. Jeff graduated from Cornell University with majors in Economics and Philosophy.

Jeff and his wife, Katy, are blessed to live with their two-year-old daughter, Abby, in Maineville, Ohio.

DAVID W MILLER (27, 30, 39-40, 41-44, 44-46, 66, 113-114, 195, 195-197)

David W. Miller, PhD serves as the Director of the Princeton University Faith & Work Initiative (http://faithandwork.princeton.edu) and as an Associate Research Scholar and Lecturer. He is also co-founder and President of The Avodah Institute. Prior to this, he spent five years at Yale University, where he was the Executive Director of the Yale Center for Faith & Culture and taught business ethics at Yale's Divinity School and School of Management. Miller also serves as an advisor to CEOs and business leaders on issues pertaining to ethics, values, leadership, and faith at work.

Miller's first book, *God at Work: The History and Promise of the Faith at Work Movement* challenges business academics and executives, as well as theologians and clergy to think differently about the place of faith at work. Prior to academia, Miller spent sixteen years in international business and finance, the latter eight of which as a senior executive based in London, and as a partner in a small private investment banking firm. With this background, he brings a unique "bilingual" perspective to his teaching, research, and corporate advisory work.

DAVID MORKEN (54-55, 141-142, 142-143, 143-146)

David Morken is president and CEO of Bandwidth.com. In 2008, Morken was named one of the *Triangle Business Journals* 40 Under 40 top business leaders. In the same year, Bandwidth made the *Inc. Magazine* 500 list for the third consecutive year as the fourth-fastest growing privately held company and the fastest-growing telecommunications company from 2002 to 2007.

In 1994, Morken co-founded the Internet's first online tax filing service, efiling. com. He was called to active duty by the Marine Corps in 1995 and served four years as a Judge Advocate, criminal prosecutor, and headquarters company commander. Morken is a graduate of the University of Notre Dame Law School and a member of the Virginia Bar Association. He received his undergraduate degree from Oral Roberts University, where he also served as president of the student body.

Morken suffers from an addiction to endurance athletics, finishing the 2008 Wasatch 100-mile Ultra-marathon in twenty-second place with a time of less than twenty-seven hours. In 2009, *Business Leader Magazine* named Morken the Healthiest CEO in The Triangle (Raleigh-Durham). He was the first finisher from North Carolina in the 2005 Ironman World Championships held in Kona, Hawaii, finishing in nine hours and forty-three minutes. Morken was a two-time member of the Marine Corps Triathlon team in 1997-98.

Morken resides in Chapel Hill with his wife Chrishelle and their six children.

WENDY MURPHY (92-93, 93-94, 148, 162, 163, 184, 207-208, 208-209)
Wendy Murphy is Managing Partner of Heidrick & Struggles' Chief Human Resources Officers Practice. Her experience in human resources both domestically and internationally, brings depth and insight into her work with her global client base. Her clients include: ABN-AMRO, Cisco, Coca-Cola, Freddie Mac, Lincoln Financial Corporation, Maersk, Incorporated, Merck, BNY Mellon, National Grid, Philips Medical Systems, PricewaterhouseCoopers, UBS, and United Airlines.

Prior to joining Heidrick & Struggles, Wendy worked in both management consulting and executive search, holding consulting positions with Organizational Dynamics, Incorporated (ODI), a global consulting and training company; Winter Wyman & Company in Boston; The Solomon-Page Group, Ltd in New York, where she served as a Group Vice President; and TMP Worldwide Executive Search, where she served as a Partner in the Global Human Resources Practice. Wendy also serves on the Advisory Board for the USC's Marshall School CEO Group and The Princeton Faith and Work Initiative.

BLAKE MYCOSKIE (125-126)
Blake is an entrepreneur and has created five businesses since college. His first was a successful national campus laundry service; his second start-up, Mycoskie Media, was purchased by Clear Channel Media. Between business ventures, Blake competed in the CBS' primetime series, *The Amazing Race*. With his sister, Paige, Blake traveled the world and came within minutes of winning the $1 million dollar grand prize.

After *The Amazing Race*, Blake attempted to create the first TV cable channel dedicated entirely to reality programming. His fourth start-up was an online driver's education school that featured hybrid cars and SUVs. After returning from a holiday in Argentina, Blake decided to sell this business to focus full-time on his latest idea, the creation of TOMS Shoes. TOMS Shoes focuses on the simple promise to give a pair of new shoes to children in need around the world with every pair sold.

Blake is an avid reader and traveler. He lives on a sailboat in Los Angeles.

DENNIS PEMBERTON (177, 200-201)

As the Managing Partner and Chief Executive Officer of Global Asset Alternatives, LLC, Dennis is responsible for crafting and implementing the vision of the company, identifying and executing investment strategies, and creating and maintaining client relationships.

Prior to forming Global Asset Alternatives, Dennis served as Managing Director-Capital Markets of Shoptaw & Garrard, LLC, a boutique investment management firm, where he oversaw research, portfolio management, fund formation, and capital raising activities. Prior to joining Shoptaw & Garrard, Dennis was affiliated with Security Capital Group, Inc. (SCG), a global real estate investment management, and research organization. Dennis has also worked for CIGNA Investment Management as an asset manager, responsible for a $300-million portfolio. Additionally, he has held positions at Lehman Brothers and the Prudential Realty Group.

Dennis has a Bachelor of Arts degree in Business Administration from Morehouse College, having graduated with honors, and a Master of Business Administration from Harvard Business School.

Dennis is active in a number of community and civic organizations, including the Woodruff Arts Center and the United Way and serves on the Board of the Sanders/Buckhead Family YMCA, the Emory University Center for Ethics, Boys & Girls Clubs of Metro Atlanta, and The Buckhead Club.

STEVE REINEMUND (58, 114, 146, 163, 201-202, 210-212)

Steve Reinemund is the Dean of Business at Wake Forest University, and Professor of Leadership and Strategy. Steve retired as Chairman of the Board of PepsiCo, Inc. in May 2007 and as Chief Executive Officer in October 2006. He is a twenty-three-year PepsiCo veteran who led the corporation as Chairman and Chief Executive from 2001 to 2006. During that period, PepsiCo's revenues increased by more than $9 billion, net income increased by seventy percent, earnings per share increased by eighty percent, its annual dividend doubled, and the company's market capitalization surpassed $100 billion. In addition to the growth of the company, Steve's legacy includes a commitment to health and wellness, diversity and inclusion, and values-based leadership.

Steve is currently a member of the board of directors of American Express, Exxon, and Marriott, and serves as a trustee on the United States Naval Academy Foundation. From 2005 to 2007, Steve was chairman of the National Minority Supplier Development Council. He served on the National Advisory Board of the Salvation Army from 1990 to 1999, and he was chairman of this board from 1996 to 1999. Steve also served on the board of The National Council of La Raza from 1992 to 2001 and was chairman of its Corporate Board of Advisors from 1992 to 1996. Steve has honorary doctorates from Bryant University and Johnson and Wales University. He did his MBA at the University of Virginia and his Bachelor of Science at the United States Naval Academy.

JEFFREY A RUSSELL (189-193)

Jeff is currently the CEO of Easy Office, a social venture providing affordable finance services to nonprofits in the US. He has served as the Executive Director for an international development nonprofit, The Momentum Group. He lived in Bangkok, Thailand for 3+ years as the Director of Supply Chain Planning for a $350-million supply chain services company. While there, he designed and implemented a back-office shared service center that handled over $250 million worth of transactions each year.

Jeff is a Georgia Tech Industrial Engineer and holds an MBA from Yale University. He and his wife, Tara, live with their two children in Boise, Idaho.

MARK L RUSSELL

(Intro, 22-23, 50, 64, 80, 106, 124, 138-139, 158-159, 174, 188, 206, 222)

Mark L. Russell is the Founder and CEO of Russell Media. Russell is a frequent public speaker and has worked as a consultant to a wide array of organizations. He is the lead editor of *Our Souls at Work* as well the author of *The Missional Entrepreneur: Principles and Practices for Business as Mission* and a co-author of *Routes and Radishes: And Other Things to Talk about at the Evangelical Crossroads.*

Russell has a PhD in intercultural studies from Asbury Theological Seminary, a Master of Divinity degree from Trinity Evangelical Divinity School, and a Bachelor of Science degree in International Business from Auburn University. His PhD thesis focused on business as mission (BAM). Mark has lived and worked in Russia, Chile, and Germany and traveled to more than seventy countries to carry out a variety of business, educational, humanitarian, and religious projects. Mark has more than sixty academic and popular publications.

Mark lives in Boise, Idaho, with his wife, Laurie and their children, Noah and Anastasia.

RICK SCHNEIDER (150-155)

Rick graduated from Harvard in 1982. He worked in political campaigns, as a campus minister, and in several high-tech sales positions in the U.S. and in Russia. In 1993 the Schneiders moved to Moscow, where Rick was Vice President of TRI and Director of the Christian Embassy, Russia.

In 2002, Rick completed his PhD in Russian political sociology before returning with his family to Yale, where he is a Senior Fellow at the Rivendell Institute. Rick travels regularly to Russia where he continues to teach on Civil Society (including the role of free market economic institutions) as an Adjunct Professor at the

Moscow State Institute of International Relations. Rick is married to Soozie Reynolds Schneider and has three delightful and talented teenagers.

TYLER SELF (94-95)

Tyler Self is the co-founder and Chief Investment Officer of Vision Research Capital Management, LP, a Dallas-based investment manager for accredited and institutional investors. In this role, Tyler oversees all investment activity of the firm and serves as Portfolio Manager of Vision Research Capital Fund, LP where he has built a track record of generating profitable returns that have significantly outperformed U.S. indices.

Prior to launching Vision Research Capital Fund in 2006, Tyler founded and served as CEO and Director of Research of Vision Research Organization, LLC, where he oversaw an independent consulting service targeting large institutional investors and hedge funds. Under Tyler's leadership, Vision Research was selected as the top overall Forensic Accounting, Quality of Earnings, and Short Idea research firm in the country.

Tyler graduated from Baylor University with a Bachelor of Business Administration. In the year of his graduation, Tyler was the only undergraduate student in the United States to receive direct admission to the Harvard Business School Master of Business Administration program. Tyler continues to support undergraduate education, serving on Southern Methodist University's Alternative Asset Management Center Advisory Board and frequently appearing at Baylor University as a guest lecturer.

Tyler is also active in the community, serving as a volunteer at West Dallas Community School, a director at Videre Microfinance Institution, and a teacher at his local church. Tyler and his wife Lauren have two daughters, Ava and Abigail.

HARRI SUNDVIK (56-57, 91, 161-162)

Harri is Managing Director and regional head of a London-based investment banking team for one of the leading global investment banking firms. He covers leading international corporations, financial institutions, and government agencies. Harri has extensive corporate finance advisory and transaction execution experience in cross-border and trans-Atlantic mergers and acquisitions, shareholder value defense and strategy work, and capital raising transactions.

Harri and his wife, Heidi, have led courses and seminars on marriage-related themes both in the UK and Finland. Harri is a proud father of three sons: Henrik, Sebastian, and Daniel. As of October 2008 Harri has completed fifty-three full marathons in his running career.

FONNY SURYA (164-166)

Fonny was born and raised in Bandung, a town approximately two hours from Jakarta, Indonesia. She moved to the United States when she was seventeen to pursue her college degree at Indiana University, Bloomington. After working for about six years both in the U.S. and in Indonesia, she decided to pursue her Master of Business Administration at the Wharton School, and is now working at a major international investment bank in Jakarta, Indonesia. Her mother was a Christian, but it wasn't until college that she started to learn more about what it means to be a Christian.

JOHN TYSON (57-58, 130, 197-200, 209-210)

The grandson of the company's founder, Tyson Foods Chairman John Tyson has worked in the company since he was a teenager, in virtually every department, from operations to sales and marketing to governmental relations. He also served as President and CEO. Tyson was the architect of the acquisition of IBP, Incorporated in 2001, which precipitated a major change in the size and scope of the company's operations. He then structured the "new" Tyson Foods based on core values that defined goals and standards for personal and professional success. A key part of these core values is that Tyson Foods strives to be a company of diverse people working together to produce food, which has been and continues to be a cornerstone that has supported the growth of the company throughout the years. John Tyson also created the company's first Executive Diversity Business Council to provide guidance on and support of inclusion and diversity. In recent years, Tyson has also been a leader in the concept and practice of providing company chaplains and the establishment of faith-friendly workplaces. A devoted father of two, Tyson is also engaged in supporting the well-being and education of youth. As such, he is actively involved in Tyson Foods' philanthropic efforts with a focus on education and hunger relief.

BONNIE WURZBACHER (36-37, 37-39, 118-120)

As Senior Vice President of Global Customer Leadership, Bonnie Wurzbacher leads the growth of the company's largest global customers and develops business strategies for key channels around the world. Previously, she was responsible for customer strategy and led the development of their global customer approach.

During her twenty-five-year tenure at The Coca-Cola Company, Wurzbacher has held various senior sales, marketing, strategy, and management positions, including Vice President, business development; Vice President, southeast area; Vice President, McDonald's; and Assistant Vice President, education market in Coca-Cola North America. She serves on the company's global advisory councils for customer and commercial leadership, women's leadership, and corporate responsibility.

Wurzbacher graduated from Wheaton College with a Bachelor of Arts degree in education in 1977 and received her Master of Business Administration in general management from Emory University in 1990. She has served on the boards of Gordon Food Service, Inc., The March of Dimes, Theatrical Outfit, The Network of Executive Women, among others, and is currently the chairperson of The Georgia Foundation of Independent Colleges.

STEVE WURZBACHER (37-39, 118-120)

Steve Wurzbacher is a Principal with Tenacity, Incorporated, the nation's leading client retention firm. He joined Tenacity in 1994 after twenty years of successful senior management, marketing, and business development experience at Aramark and Procter & Gamble.

Along with direct client engagements for Tenacity, he serves as the firm's Chief Operating Officer and manages key planning and brand development functions. In addition, he is a well-known speaker on the subject of client relationship management.

Steve serves on the Governing Board of The Capital City Club in Atlanta and serves as lay leader for the WorkLife ministry at Peachtree Presbyterian Church in Atlanta.

KIMBERLY HAYDEN YERINO (131-134)

Kimberly Hayden Yerino is an alumna of the Yale School of Management, graduating in May of 2009 with a Master of Business Administration. She now works as a Senior Analyst for a Fortune 500 diversified financial services company with major operations in Connecticut. She is also currently the InterVarsity Graduate and Faculty Ministries volunteer at the Yale School of Management. Kim lives in New Haven with her husband and best friend, Christopher, who is working on a PhD in Electrical Engineering at Yale. Her favorite color is purple and one of her favorite women in the Bible is Lydia (see Acts 16:11-15).

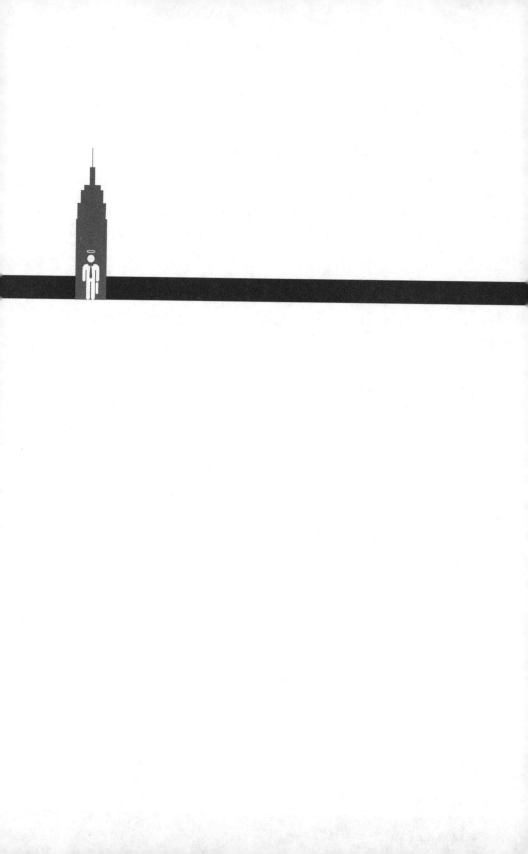

OUR SOULS AT WORK
TEAM

OUR SOULS AT WORK TEAM
(listed alphabetically)

SANDI FUNKHOUSER

Sandi is a seasoned writer, trainer, speaker, and certified e-learning specialist. During her career, Sandi has enjoyed the privilege of speaking and working on five continents, in ministry, and in the corporate world. Her work in "corporate America" allowed her to experience the inception, growth, and maturity of several companies and to help several hundred small business owners find their footing in the business world.

Sandi has written for both corporate and faith-based publications and is the author of the book, *The Doorkeeper: In the King's Presence*. She is also the managing partner for Three Sisters Communication, LLC and works with Price Associates in Boise, Idaho. Sandi has been certified as a Professional Behaviors and Values Analyst and is a life coach.

She served as an associate editor on the *Our Souls at Work* project.

MELISSA KILLIAN

Melissa Killian has a BA in International Relations and a BS in Business. She continued to pursue her passion for intercultural human resource and product development in graduate school while living in Athens, Greece. After earning her MBA in International Management, she worked in training and development for the university before joining Christian Business Leaders International as their partner and product development coordinator. Helping pastors, speakers, and all types of leaders identify and develop their best messages was a natural fit, and as a pre-journalism major, has found ghostwriting to be a natural gift.

In the past five years, she and her husband Rick have launched a nonprofit to serve the youth in their area and are currently working with the college prayer movement. They are the proud parents of two high achieving teenagers, Hannah and Caleb.

She served as a copy editor on the *Our Souls at Work* project.

RICK KILLIAN

Rick Killian is a freelance ghostwriter, editor, and consultant for Killian Creative (www.killiancreative.com), which he started with his wife in 2001. Rick Killian earned his BA from Willamette University, majoring in English and minoring in math, clinical psychology, and religion. After college, Rick served two years in the Peace Corps, which is also where he and Melissa met. The two taught and ministered in Greece for eight years and after returning to the States, began working in Christian publishing.

Rick began his publishing career in editorial development at Albury Publishing where he oversaw production of the Gold Medallion nominated and bestselling collaboration between dc talk and The Voice of the Martyrs, *Jesus Freaks*. His first project as a freelance writer was ghostwriting its sequel, *Jesus Freaks: Revolutionaries*, and has collaborated on nearly fifty titles, which have sold over 2.5 million copies. Two of those titles hit #1 and #4 on *New York Times Best Sellers Lists*.

He served as a copy editor on the *Our Souls at Work* project.

LAURIE D RUSSELL

Laurie D. Russell is the Chief Creative Officer of Russell Media. She has numerous publications to her credit. Laurie has worked for several law firms, a marketing company and a couple of publishing houses. She is a graduate of Moody Bible Institute and has served as Stewardship Coordinator for the Boise Chapter of A Rocha, a Christian conservation organization. Laurie has lived and worked in Russia, Chile, and Germany and has traveled to around forty countries on a variety of projects. She lives with her husband, Mark, their two children, Noah and Anastasia, their two dogs, Louie and Gracie, and their two cats, Molly and Ferris, in Boise, Idaho.

She served as an associate editor on the *Our Souls at Work* project.

MARK L RUSSELL

Mark served as lead editor on the *Our Souls at Work* project. To read his full bio, see the list of contributors.

ANDREA NAGY SMITH

Andrea Nagy Smith is a case writer for the Yale School of Management. She has produced cases covering a variety of organizations, including Boston Scientific, the New York Police Department, American Greetings, Agora SA, Mercy Corps, the Connecticut Department of Transportation, the Guggenheim Museum, and the Polaroid Corporation.

For Yale's interdisciplinary course on Faith & Globalization, she produced ten online case studies on topics including the decline of Christianity in Sweden and the rise of Christianity in China. She is also an editor of the *New Oxford American Dictionary*. She holds a PhD in English from the University of Virginia.

She served as an associate editor on the *Our Souls at Work* project.

DREW STEFFEN

Whether it is the buildings we live and work in or the books we pick up off the shelf to read, Drew operates on the premise that God has inspired design all around us and excellent presentation is crucial to every endeavor. Educated as an architect at Iowa State University, Drew sharpened his skills designing skyscrapers around the world before attending Yale University, where he earned both a Masters of Architecture and a MBA.

While at Yale, Drew took part in creating the international touring museum exhibit *Eero Saarinen: Shaping the Future*, and co-edited and published *Future Proofing*, a book chronicling strategies to create cities with long-term viability. Drew specializes in commercial real estate development in Houston, Texas, where he lives with his wife Kristy, and three boys.

He served as the graphic designer and layout specialist on the *Our Souls at Work* project. Sola scriptura, sola gratia, solus christus, sola fide, soli deo gloria.

NICOLE WONG

Nicole (www.nicolecwong.com) is an award-winning business journalist who has worked on the reporting staffs of *The Washington Post, The Boston Globe,* and *San Jose Mercury News,* and on a freelance basis for VentureBeat.com and WalletPop.com. She's reported extensively on management and workplace issues, technology companies and tech culture, travel and transportation, education and youth health issues, and city government.

Nicole also works one-on-one with business professionals as a writing coach and has taught high school students as an assigning editor at the Mosaic Urban Journalism Workshop in Silicon Valley. She's spending the 2009-2010 academic year as a Knight-Bagehot Fellow in Economics and Business at Columbia Business School and Columbia Journalism School. Nicole earned a BS from the Walter A. Haas School of Business at the University of California, Berkeley and will receive a Masters of Science in Journalism from Columbia University when her fellowship ends in May 2010.

She served as an associate editor on the *Our Souls at Work* project.

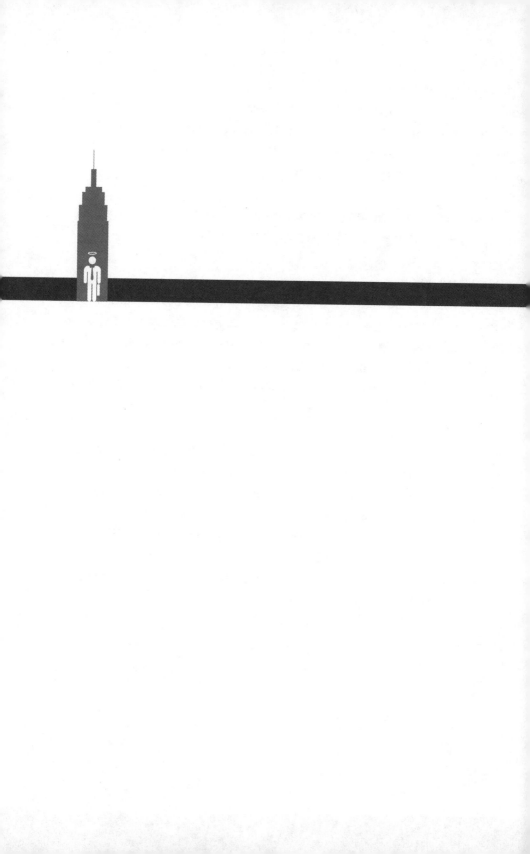

OUR SOULS AT WORK
APPENDIX

appendix A

THE MBA OATH

Preamble

As a manager, my purpose is to serve the greater good by bringing people and resources together to create value that no single individual can build alone. Therefore, I will seek a course that enhances the value my enterprise can create for society over the long term. I recognize my decisions can have far-reaching consequences that affect the well-being of individuals inside and outside my enterprise, today and in the future. As I reconcile the interests of different constituencies, I will face difficult choices.

Therefore, I promise:

I will act with utmost integrity and pursue my work in an ethical manner. My personal behavior will be an example of integrity, consistent with the values I publicly espouse.

I will safeguard the interests of my shareholders, co-workers, customers, and the society in which we operate. I will endeavor to protect the interests of those who may not have power, but whose well-being is contingent on my decisions.

I will manage my enterprise in good faith, guarding against decisions and behavior that advance my own narrow ambitions but harm the enterprise and the people it serves. The pursuit of self-interest is the vital engine of a capitalist economy, but unbridled greed can be just as harmful. I will oppose corruption, unfair discrimination, and exploitation.

I will understand and uphold, both in letter and in spirit, the laws and contracts governing my own conduct and that of my enterprise. If I find laws that are unjust, antiquated, or unhelpful I will not brazenly break, ignore, or avoid them; I will seek civil and acceptable means of reforming them.

I will take responsibility for my actions, and I will represent the performance and risks of my enterprise accurately and honestly. My aim will not be to distort the truth, but to transparently explain it and help people understand how decisions that affect them are made.

I will develop both myself and other managers under my supervision so that the profession continues to grow and contribute to the well-being of society. I will consult colleagues and others who can help inform my judgment and will continually invest in staying abreast of the evolving knowledge in the field, always remaining open to innovation. I will mentor and look after the education of the next generation of leaders.

I will strive to create sustainable economic, social, and environmental prosperity worldwide. Sustainable prosperity is created when the enterprise produces an output in the long run that is greater than the opportunity cost of all the inputs it consumes.

I will be accountable to my peers and they will be accountable to me for living by this oath. I recognize that my stature and privileges as a professional stem from the respect and trust that the profession as a whole enjoys, and I accept my responsibility for embodying, protecting, and developing the standards of the management profession so as to enhance that trust and respect.

This oath I make freely, and upon my honor.

If you have a MBA or are in the final year of your MBA go to
http://mbaoath.org/sign-the-oath to sign the oath.

HOWARD DAHL LETTERS

2800 7th Avenue North / Fargo, North Dakota 58102
Telephone: (701) 280-1260

January 14, 1988

TO: Concord, Inc. Suppliers

Concord has just completed a most difficult year. It was a year of great uncertainty and a year of major adjustments. On November 11, 1987, we wrote you telling of our great difficulty in securing a bank line, and we said we would communicate at year end.

During 1987 our retail sales dropped approximately 50%. There are three or four major reasons for this. As a result, the amount of equipment we had on floorplan was excessive and at the lower sales levels our operating expenses were too high. We had averaged over $5.0 million of retail activity between 1983 and 1986, a period in which we were slightly profitable each year. Our forecast for 1987 was for no sales growth or decline, but sales dropped below $3.0 million.

With our inability to secure an adequate bank line we had to make some major decisions. We knew our top priority was to eliminate our field inventory. On October 15th, we put a 15% discount program in place and have seen approximately 50% of our field inventory retail.

Our main bank demanded full payment of our outstanding balance to them in late November. We had a balance of $900,000 with them in June and have since got that balance to a level where we believe we can meet the January 29th deadline of paying them out in full. Our floorplan lenders have given us complete support in the liquidation of the floorplan, and our major suppliers have been of great encouragement by showing forbearance.

We are now at a point where we can see a good solid game plan for 1988 and beyond. We have made necessary reductions in staff and other operating expenses to where our breakeven point is below $4.0 million of sales, and our cash flow breakeven point is $3.0 million. To reach this level we eliminated our vice president level and a number of other positions in our organization. For those of you particularly who have dealt with Bob Glas and John Walko over the past ten years, you know what a painful decision that was. Both of them are talking to a number of companies about possible employment. In our new structure our Purchasing Manager will be Dean Paulsen and our Chief Engineer will be Mike Smette. Your inquiries can be directed to them.

letter from Howard Dahl, January 1988

We have excellent sales activity right now, and we anticipate a very strong spring. Indeed we have presold 30% of our build for the year already and anticipate that number to be 50% by January 31st. In addition, we can look into 1989 and see approximately 35% of our production directed toward a product we are building for Case-IH.

Perhaps the main reason we are optimistic about sales can be found by reading the attached summary from the Saskatchewan Department of Agriculture. We have been tested many times in side-by-side comparisons with one or two other seeders and have emerged the better seeder. But never has a comparison been done by a governmental agency comparing 15 seeders. As you can see, we had a 47.5% better yield than the average. This study alone has created untold excitement. Our machine consistently performs and has a chance to emerge as the preeminent seeding machine in every area.

But what about our obligation to you? We are feverishly working on getting the documentation prepared for a couple banks to secure a new bank line. At the end of January we will be without a bank line and in a position of having about $2.0 million of collateral to pledge to a bank. The uncertainty that remains is whether or not we can get a bank line, and if we can, what the size of that bank line will be. We hope to have something in place by mid to late February.

In the interim, we have talked with many of you and have gotten a variety of responses as to how you want to handle our obligation to you. We could benefit immeasurably in our cashflow planning if you could let us know specifically what would be your first and second preference out of the variety of options you have collectively suggested to me.

OPTIONS I PREFER:

1. Simply wait until you secure a bank line and talk again at that point.

2. Set up a payment schedule now for the next 12 months.

3. Convert the amount owing to a preferred stock.

4. If Concord would come up with the money, settle the account quickly at approximately $.50 on the dollar.

5. Concord has a variety of items in inventory that are not going to be used in the near term, as well as having some excess equipment. Would you be interested in some sort of barter arrangement?

    1st Choice is #_____

    2nd Choice is #_____

I will personally be handling all supplier relations and ask that you do not hesitate to call me to ask any questions about this letter or general questions about Concord.

We appreciate your willingness to carefully consider our situation and how we can best emerge from this quagmire we have been in.

Sincerely,

Howard A Dahl

Howard A. Dahl
President & CEO

km

Crystal Lake Zero Till Seeding Demo.

Seeding Date: June 4, 1987   Harvest Date: October 10, 1987

Make and Model of Seeder	Combined size of plot(ac.)	Yield .lbs	Weight Bu.	Moisture at time combined	Yield Bu./Ac.	Variance from the average	Yield Banded Fertil.	Yield\ topdres Urea
Concord 3310	.204	672.00	11.20	19.40	54.90	47.50%	54.90	
Morris	.204	590.00	9.83	14.80	48.20	29.50%	48.20	
Leon 1080T	.204	524.00	8.73	21.50	42.80	14.99%		42.80
Haybuster 1000	.204	483.00	8.05	15.20	39.50	6.13%	39.50	
John Deere 655	.204	464.50	7.74	15.00	37.90	1.83%		37.90
Degelman	.170	380.00	6.33	14.80	37.20	-.05%	37.20	
Edwards Modif.	.178	380.00	6.33	14.80	35.60	-4.35%		35.60
Wilrich 4153	.204	430.80	7.18	17.60	35.20	-5.43%		35.20
Case IH	.204	420.90	7.00	20.00	34.30	-7.85%		34.30
Bourgault 2115	.204	418.20	6.97	22.50	34.20	-8.11%		34.20
GT	.204	412.10	6.90	16.30	33.80	-9.19%		33.80
Haybuster 8000	.193	378.20	6.30	16.30	32.80	-11.88%		32.80
Amazone NT 375	.204	354.50	5.91	23.40	29.00	-22.08%		29.00
Blanchard	.204	314.20	5.24	18.80	25.70	-30.95%		25.70
Field Total	2.785	6222.400	103.710					
Plot Aver	.20	444.46	7.41	17.89	37.22		44.95	34.13

concord inc.

2800 7th Avenue North/Fargo, North Dakota 58102
Telephone: (701) 280-1260   FAX# 701 280-0706

May 8, 1989

Dear valued supplier:

After 18 months of working on new financing, a day of reckoning
has come. The SBA has formally approved our loan.   Before any
moneys will be released, however, we need you to return the
attached form which spells out precisely what you will receive as
full settlement for the monies we owe you.   No checks will be
sent to any suppliers until we receive reponses from everyone.
Thus, it is in your best interest to return this form as quickly
as possible.

I, perhaps, need to reiterate a couple items for your benefit.
It is not, nor ever has been our intention to take advantage of
you.   If it had been, we would have filed a Chaper 11 one year
ago. Very likely, no unsecured creditors would have received
more that $.10 on the dollar if that had happened. As it is, we
have been able to keep buying product from many of you on a cash
basis, and are now able to pay you $.50 toward the past
obligations.

As we continue our rebuilding efforts, we are very hopeful that
you will be more than compensated from Concord by receiving
future business from a sound company. I am so very aware of the
tremendous rebuilding job we have to do in the marketplace, for
many farmers have looked at us as either being on our deathbed or
already in the morgue.

Please don't hesitate to call if you have any questions. We must
hear from all of you before the funds will be released.

Sincerely,

Howard A. Dahl

letter from Howard Dahl, May 1989

concord
inc.

2800 7th Avenue North/Fargo, North Dakota 58102
Telephone: (701) 280-1260   FAX# 701 280-0706

I hereby acknowedge that we will accept _____ as
payment in full from Concord, Inc. for all indebtebtedness that
exists at this time.

Dated: May ___, 1989

_____NAME

_____TITLE

_____COMPANY

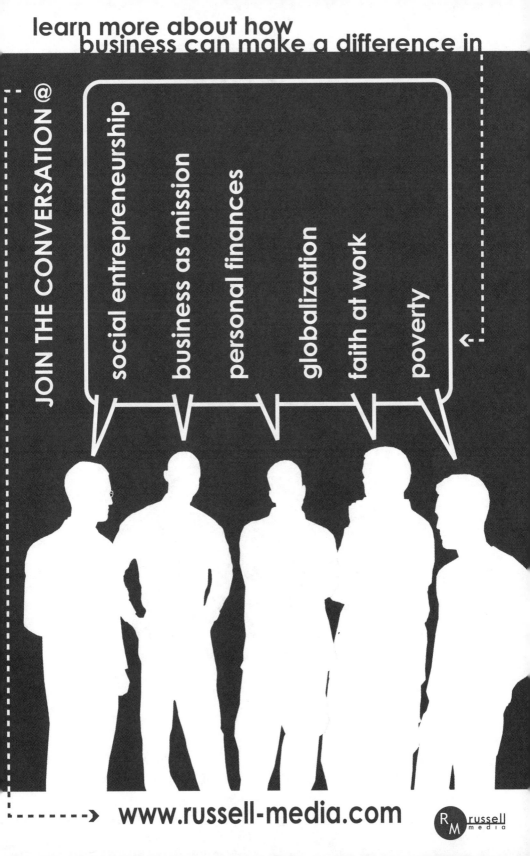

find out more about Business As Mission (BAM), through . . .

the MISSIONAL ENTREPRENEUR
Principles and Practices for Business as Mission

www.russell-media.com

Check out the annual
Believers in Business Conference
at Yale

http://students.som.yale.edu/clubs/christian/index.html

NO TREES WERE HARMED
IN THE MAKING OF THIS BOOK

OK, so a few
did need to make the ultimate sacrifice.

In order to steward God's good creation,
we are partnering with *Plant With Purpose*, to plant
a tree for every tree that paid the price for the printing of
this book.

www.russell-media.com

www.plantwithpurpose.org